AF611034

The IMMEDIATE → Discography

The First 20 Years

The IMMEDIATE → Discography

The First 20 Years

Mark Jones

The Immediate Discography: The First 20 Years
Mark Jones

This edition published 2016 by The Record Press

The Record Press is an imprint of Bristol Folk Publications
www.bristol–folk.co.uk

ISBN 13: 978–1–909953–57–4

Copyright © Mark Jones 2016

Jacket design copyright © The Record Press 2016
Digital layout and realisation by The Record Press

NOTICE OF RIGHTS
All rights reserved. The right of Mark Jones, to be identified as the Author of this work has been asserted in accordance with the Copyrights, Designs and Patents Act 1988. No part of this book may be reprinted or reproduced or utilised or transmitted in any form or by any means, electronic or mechanical, including photocopy, recording, or any information storage and retrieval system, including the Internet, now known or hereafter invented, without permission in writing from the copyright holder.

CONTENTS

In Memoriam:

The sad news of Keith Emerson's death on 11 March 2016 broke just as this book was about to go to print. Emerson, of course, was a major player within the Immediate camp. His band, The Nice, was originally formed as P.P. Arnold's backing band and went on to be a hugely–influential group in its own right. The band's third album, their last for the original Immediate label, was one of those turning points for me and my love of The Nice and the Small Faces in particular is probably the reason why this book exists. Emerson went on to near world domination with ELP but IMSP 026, *Nice*, remains, for me, Emerson's finest vinyl moment. Time to give it yet another spin, I think.

FOREWORD

First, some trumpet blowing, whilst this current book was in preparation, one of the earlier books in the *Great British Record Label* series was nominated for an international academic award. It's nice to discover that you're doing something right – in fact, to discover that you are leading the field in terms of research and presentation of research findings and that others are following your lead. And it happened just at the point that I was about to give up because of lack of support in terms of adequate sales. So, a mere thirty–seven years after I first started to document the label's releases, here are the fruits of my Immediate–flavoured discographical labours. This almost didn't make it to publication. Thank the award nomination for this book becoming a reality.

So what was the award and which book was nominated? Well, the book is *The B&C Discography: 1968 to 1975* and the nomination was for the Association for Recorded Sound Collections Award for Excellence in Historical Recorded Sound Research. I didn't win, but just being nominated was a surprise.

To get back on track, what was it about Immediate that has assured the label a set of fervent followers down the years? Well, for one thing, Immediate's acts were hip (even Jimmy Tarbuck, back then), and in a couple of cases, ground–breaking. Not only that, but the marketing tactics used were different to anything that had gone before.

The dream, of course, ended in bankruptcy and the label has been exploited in one way or another ever since, with the music licensed to all number of companies in the intervening years. But the label's identity seems to remain intact. People that released one non–selling single on Immediate in 1966, for example, are still, in record collecting terms, remembered as 'Immediate artists' no matter what else they've done in the intervening forty–odd years.

As to the times, Andrew Oldham's two 'autobiographies', *Stoned* and *2Stoned*, seem to present a man directing his own film, the star to everyone else's support and cameo roles. The movie set was that of Swinging Sixties London, juxtaposed with the Burgess–like ultra–violence of London's gangland alter ego, with the scenes no doubt played out to a soundtrack of The Andrew Oldham Orchestra And Chorus.

In a way, Immediate was the first punk label. It came out and said that it didn't need the established industry (except to press, distribute and advertise the records, of course), and would be successful on its own terms. And Immediate's own terms consisted of making up the rules as it went along, and breaking them whenever convenient; a maverick label, run by mavericks, releasing music as smartly–honed and sharp as Andrew Oldham's own wardrobe.

Even without rose–tinted spectacles, the whole seemed so much more than the sum of its parts. The only real trouble with Immediate was that it didn't have a clue how to exploit the US music industry – and that was really its downfall. Well, that and near limitless financial extravagence. Still, what's money for, if not to spend?

To move inward to a more personal view, my first tastes in music in the early to mid–60s were those of my older sister, whose Saturday job money went on a memorable series of releases by the Stones, Pretty Things, Who, Small Faces, Spencer Davis Group and various Tamla greats. From this frenzy of excellent music I can remember the exact moment that I fell in love with Immediate – and it was a fall for the whole image as embodied in the Small Faces' first release for the label. It was a combination of the group, the song, the sound, the label design and the sleeve. I was four–years–old when I heard *Here Come the Nice*, that Sunday afternoon in March 1967. It still seems like yesterday, whilst last week was such a long time ago.

Yes, it wasn't just the music, it was the whole package. The sleeve was bright – gleaming white – with sharp, angular, mod lettering and the label was a shining lilac colour. The rest of my sister's records looked drab against this new addition. Labels such as Parlophone, Columbia, Brunswick, Decca, Tamla and so on were uniformly black or dark blue. Pye, although red, was a drab red. Fontana and Reaction were less drab but still dark. The feel was that of traditional British companies still running along austerity lines – if dark and drab is good enough for us adults, then it's more than good enough for you children. Immediate was definitely not dark and drab. It was both eye– and ear–catching. What's more, children no longer knew their place – there'll be be no more 'seen and not heard', thank you very much (just like with every generation, really).

The sixties seemed to me to be all about singles. I remember individual singles arriving because they got played (to death) either early Saturday evenings (whilst my sister's nail varnish dried in advance of her heading out to see various R&B legends at Bristol's Colston Hall or Corn Exchange) or post–prandially on Sunday afternoons, by this time on the posh, new radiogram, when my sister's hip friends would descend on far–out Shirehampton (sometimes from as far away as France) to enjoy endless cups of tea and where I would occasionally have a surrepticious 'drag' on someone or other's Players Number 6 and spend the rest of the afternoon feeling sick. Great days.

As for LPs; I don't remember any of the early ones being bought – they just seemed to be there. The ones I remember are my sister's copies of the Hollies' *For Certain Because*, plus the Monkees' first LP and *Head Quarters*, those and my brother's first three LPs, which sat proudly on the mantelpiece above the fireplace in the sitting room. These were Dylan's first album along with *The Freewheeling Bob Dylan* and *John Mayall's Bluesbreakers with Eric Clapton*. The first one I remember seeing arrive was my brother's copy of Humble Pie's *As Safe As Yesterday Is*. Yes, Immediate again.

Anyway, back to the age–old question. Why no pictures? All I'll say on that score is that the copyright situation as regards Immediate is a little *complex*. This is an example of understatement, by the way. If there was any way that I could guarantee that this book would not be sold outside of the UK (or if I could guarantee that it would be sold anywhere in the world except the UK), then all would be well. Unfortunately, thanks to an equally complex distribution model over which I, as author, have no control, I can make no such guarantee, so you'll have to put up with a much cheaper book than the one it might have been. Check out the exemplary *45cat.com* for 7" label and sleeve scans and *discogs.com* for LP and other sleeve illustrations. This is called blended learning!

Thanks to: Barry Green (curator of Charly's Immediate archive for additions, corrections, confirmations and more); Rob Caiger (Charly Label Manager); Simon Lindsay (Universal Music Group/Sanctuary Legal and Business Affairs).

GROUND RULES

A lot has been written about Immediate and the better–known of its two owners so, with this in mind, it is worth pointing out what this book is and what it is not, along with where to go if you want to find out more about the artists and personalities. First and foremost this is a discography; so we're interested in which records were released and when, with full supporting cast of documentation of original label design and distributor information. The organisational history is here to support the discography, rather than to be entertaining in its own right. Basically, this book is concerned with Immediate as a record company and is not necessarily concerned with the hype surrounding the label and its owners, except inasmuch as that hype was a deliberate strategy.

Hype a deliberate strategy? In 1965? In the UK? This was something new in Britain and, in UK terms, Immediate was probably the earliest and most successful example (for a while) of entrepreneurial brand building and image positioning through storytelling and self–mythologizing. The Americans could do this sort of thing in their sleep – just think Hollywood – but the British couldn't conceive of doing things this way. It took the all the brash insecurity of youth to break the rules – and the fact that the hype didn't break much ice in the US probably says something, though buggered if I know what.

Be that as it may, those who want a more colourful and much more in–depth take on the company and the people are pointed toward the *Labels Unlimited* series book, *Immediate*, by Simon Spence (Black Dog Publishing, 2008 – updated edition in much nicer jacket design, 2012). Spence's book is almost the complete opposite of this book and deals happily with the artists and personalities (not always the same people) to present a lurid history of the label. One or two minor errors notwithstanding, it is a great read, though the discography section is a bit light on detail. On the one hand you get a particularly good selection of record sleeves, memorabilia and photos but, on the other, those with a liking for methodical lists are left a bit wanting – hence the gap in the market for this slender (and cheaper) volume.

You are also pointed to *Stoned* and *2Stoned*, two books published under Andrew Loog Oldham's name, although, perhaps surprisingly, these barely mention Immediate. The material relating to Immediate gathered during research and writing for the two Oldham books is what makes up the majority of Simon Spence's book, above. What Oldham's two books do, though, is to give a very good idea of the man and of the times.

What this book does, then, is to avoid, for the most part, things that can be found in the above three mentioned books and, instead, complements these. The expectation is, in any case, that you will read this alongside these other books so as to get a richer picture. Hence a shorter organisational history than with other Record Press discographies – but, as I've been told more than once, who reads the organsisational history anyway? Well, those nominating books for international awards; that's who.

ORGANISATIONAL HISTORY

Pre–Immediate

If we peek out of the Tardis in the couple of years leading up to Immediate's incorporation, what do we see? Britain is moving slowly out of a post–war, austerity mind–set and youth is waking up to how much freedom and spending power it has. There is near enough full employment and parents, teachers and politicians are, as always, unhip and square. The worlds of fashion, art, music, film – in fact everything – seem to be converging and London is suddenly the most 'in' city in the world. Forget Rome. Forget Paris. Forget New York. London is the place to be. The Beatles are still loveable mop tops. The Rolling Stones will soon explode in the public consciousness, not so much as a group, but more as a moral outrage. As Chris Andrews might have said, Bill Haley and Chubby Checker are so yesterday, man. This new–fangled beat music is giving adults a headache and the kids love it.

Andrew Loog Oldham and Tony Calder came together in 1963 as Image, the UK music industry's first independent musical artiste public relations company. Prior to this, Oldham had worked for Mary Quant during the day and at Ronnie Scott's and the Flamingo Club at nights. Sleep, evidently, was for other people. Calder had worked briefly for Decca (and Jimmy Saville) in the very early 1960s before moving into PR.

By showing themselves to be more innovative and motivated than the PR departments of major record labels, Oldham and Calder quickly picked up accounts for Brian Epstein's stable of artists and also those for Manchester's Kennedy Street Enterprises. Between these two companies, Image handled PR for, not just The Beatles, but Gerry and the Pacemakers, The Hollies, Herman's Hermits, Wayne Fontana and the Mindbenders, Freddie and the Dreamers and more – in other words, the cream of the modern beat group crop. They also handled The Beach Boys in the UK, which partially explains how that group's compositions ended up being published, for a while at least, by Immediate Music.

Oldham and Calder were, if you like, image designers and the deal was that they sold themselves as well as their artists. The sleeve notes to *16 Hip Hits* by The Andrew Oldham Orchestra And Chorus probably say it all:

> Born aeons of light years too early – a legend in his own lifetime – a national institution in his industry – these are just a smattering of phrases used to describe the many faces of Andrew Loog Oldham. Part–magician, part Brains Trust, this twenty–year–old citizen of the world has carefully sprinkled his own special golden Midas dust on the careers of such household luxuries as The Rolling Stones, Gene Pitney, Marianne Faithfull, and other citizens of the tinsel fishbowl. His skills range from Image Builder to Orchestra and Chorus Conductor...

Oldham is best remembered as The Rolling Stones' manager, but the fact that he is remembered in this respect at all is down to his designing an image for himself as well as for his group. He made sure that he was as newsworthy as the band he managed and an aid in this was in securing his own weekly column in *Disc And Music Echo*. He was always on hand too to provide his (usually controversial) opinion for the papers. In this way he made sure that he was news and that anything that he planned was news as well.

The idea for an independent label came out of Oldham's numerous visits to the US on Rolling Stones business. US independents held a large proportion of market share in their home country but didn't seem to get the same break in the UK. Immediate came out of the wish to control the destiny of music, not just its creation. As Simon Spence's *Immediate* book states:

> Calder and Oldham both recall Immediate coming into life some time in July 1965. In the back seats of [one of] Oldham's new motors ... Immediate was born on the way to a television recording of *Ready Steady Go!* ... [Oldham's driver] screeched the Lincoln to a stop and Calder ran into a pay phone box to call the head of Philips, Leslie Gould, demanding he backed their vision for Immediate.

Immediate

Oldham's liking for US independent record labels and his dislike for the bureaucratic nature of the UK record industry both came to the surface in an article, 'Oldham Hits Out', written for *Disc And Music Echo* in early August (exact issue unknown):

> ...many readers have written in and said that if I was so disturbed by the state of the existing record companies why didn't I do something about it. I have! ... On the twentieth of this month ... my own record company, Immediate Records, is to be launched ... [and] will operate in the same way as any good small independent in America, with the accent on promotion and product and not board meetings.

In retrospect it can be viewed as amusing that the above article goes on to state that Immediate would never release more than two singles a week, so as to be able to properly promote all releases, before going on to describe the first *three* releases, all of which were to be issued the same day. Later that month, *Billboard*, described the launch of Immediate in the following terms:

> The details of Oldham's own disk firm, Immediate Records, have still to be unveiled but it is known that the product will be pressed and released by Philips on Oldham's own label. The initial release was timed for this week and was to have been a Bert Berns recording by American group, the McCoys – a disk the producer picked up on his recent visit to the U.S. The second will be a Jimmy Page production; the third a record Oldham has made himself, by the new British [sic] girl singer, Niko [sic].[1]

This news may have come to *Billboard* fresh from the horse's mouth because Oldham was in the US with Mick Jagger and Keith Richards with the various intentions of setting up a new outlet for Rolling Stones' records in the US, looking for further US independent label material to licence for UK release on Immediate and for a possible outlet for Immediate product in the US. A week later, in the same paper, Jimmy Page had mysteriously – and erroneously – turned into Larry Page, but otherwise *Billboard* was still on–message. Meanwhile, in the same article, more details had been forthcoming about the new Immediate label:

> Partnering Oldham in the venture is 24–year–old Tony Calder, ex–manager of Marianne Faithfull, who quit the previous partnership with a producer because of a disagreement ... Immediate records is based at 138–147 Ivor Court, London, N.W. 1.[2]

It's worth noting that the above address was also that as used for Rolling Stones business. Also on board with Oldham and Calder at the start of things were Philip Wainwright, ex–EMI, who joined Immediate as Press Officer, and Tony King, ex–Decca, who joined as Promotion Manager. King didn't stay long and left to join George Martin's AIR Productions at the end of February 1966, based on the promise of moving into production[3]. Coincidentally, in September 1965, *Billboard* stated that Immediate and AIR were two of the most significant happenings in the UK music business during 1965[4].

Retailers were sent a press sheet ahead of the first three releases, which were scheduled for issue on Friday, 20 August 1965. Oldham's antipathy to the way in which mainstream record companies were run shone through and this can only make you wonder how Decca and other major labels did business in the early to mid–1960s.

> Dear Retailer, We would like to introduce you to a new company representing a new growth in the record industry in Britain – Immediate Records whose premise of operation is to sell tomorrow's sound today with tomorrow's methods of selling...[Immediate Records is] a company with a young progressive approach to producing records and selling them. It will be our policy to only put out releases that will be promoted by every means possible, contrary to the policy of the major labels in this country. Should any of you wish to know more about our company or have any queries we are not in the board room upstairs with twelve directors on their death beds – we are here on the telephone selling records at Ambassador 1811. Just ask for either Mr. Andrew Loog Oldham or Mr. Tony Calder.

The first record released by Immediate, *Hang On Sloopy*, by The McCoys, was already in the *Billboard Hot 100* in the US and, according to that paper, achieved hit status in the UK in the first two days after release, going on to notch up sales of 35,000 copies in the following two weeks[5]. Bang Record's owner, Bert Berns, who had licenced the record to Immediate, was reported as being satisfied with the way that Oldham had pushed the single straight into the UK charts and said that he had confidence in Philip's backing (meaning that company's marketing of Immediate product)[6].

In October, *Billboard* advised that The McCoys would be in the UK in December 1965 along with The Strangeloves, another group licensed by Bang to Immediate, for a two week promotional tour[7] – this to coincide with the release of Immediate's first LP. Tony Calder was trusted with looking after Immediate on his own for a bit because, at the end of October, Oldham accompanied The Rolling Stones to the US for a two month stay for touring and recording[8].

1966 began with the good news, from the point of view of Immediate, that despite a downturn in the numbers of singles sold in 1965, independent record companies run by independent producers – Immediate and Shel Talmy's Planet were the companies named – were now in a position of relative strength within the industry. Whilst not "anticipat[ing] a rash of [independent labels] in 1966" EMI executive, Geoffrey Bridge, went on to say:

> The difficulties which prevented these labels to arise in the past have been twofold: getting exposure for the product and distribution. Now pirate radio has provided these producers with all the exposure they need ... they still have to get distribution and I don't think the major factors will be irresponsible in granting this.[9]

In other words, the independents, no matter how innovative and go–ahead, still needed the existing industry infrastructure to get to market and if there was money to be made out of them in this endeavour, then the major labels would certainly help the independents.

In late January 1966, Oldham's US Business Manager, Allen Klein, who ran Oldham's US music publishing company, Gideon Music, had come over to the UK to discuss existing offers from US labels to handle Immediate in the US. Meanwhile, the company was orchestrating a sales campaign – "England Swings" – to back up the release of the next three LPs, planned for March release. These included *Today's Pop Symphony*, by the Aranbee Pop Symphony Orchestra, *The Wonderful World of Sam Cooke* and Mark Murphy's *Who Can I Turn To*. The Cooke album was put together by Klein from his collection of previously unreleased Cooke recordings[10].

The above source went on to say that Immediate had just signed Goldie from the US all–girl group, Goldie and the Gingerbreads, and that both Aranbee Pop Symphony Orchestra and Sam Cooke singles were scheduled for release on 11 February. Plans must have changed because neither single appeared, if, indeed, the intention to release them was ever anything more than an idle Oldham fantasy.

To this backdrop of new signings and releases the company moved offices as from 1, August from N.W. 1 to Armward House at the rather more hip 63–69, New Oxford Street address. On records and in letters the building found itself renamed as "Immediate House", which must have pleased the postal services until they got used to it. Contact details were as follows: Telex – 27655; telephone – 01 240 3377; cables – IMMEDCORD LONDON; telegrams – IMMEDCORD LONDON W.C.1.

In April, *Billboard* revealed that Oldham had flown over to the US to reacquire the US publishing company, Immediate Music, which he'd sold to Dan and Bob Crewe on a previous visit. The cost was not revealed, but based on the fact that Immediate Music owned the copyrights to such songs as *(I Can't Get No) Satisfaction*, which not only sold silly numbers of copies by The Rolling Stones, but was also a hit in the US by Otis Redding, the price was not going to be trivial. Allen Klien & Co. took over administration of the company, to bring Immediate Music and Gideon Music under the same roof[11].

Back in the UK, 28, July, 1966, saw an unprecedented event. Chris Farlowe's cover of the Rolling Stones' *Out of Time*, hit number 1 in the UK charts. This was the first time that a single by an independent label had reached the top spot in the UK[12]. However, Immediate's UK success could not be replicated in the far bigger US market because the label didn't yet have a US distributor. Therefore, Oldham flew to the US in August with the duel intention of settling the world assignments of his Immediate Music publishing company as well as negotiating to licence *Out of Time* to MGM for non–UK sales[13].

The negotiations with MGM, however, lead to nothing but occasional one–off licensing deals. On the plus side, the same month saw The Beach Boys' Brian Wilson in talks with Immediate Music and EMI about projection of the Beach Boys in Europe in advance of their European tour[14]. Prior to the setting up of Immediate, Oldham and Calder had handled the group's PR in the UK in Image. Now that they had both a record label and a music publishing company, the latter of which handled the Beach Boys in the UK, it was not purely down to coincidence that the Immediate roster started to cover Beach Boys songs rather a lot. Immediate also put out sheet music versions of various Beach Boys songs to pull in further income and, somehow (probably through Allan Klein), gained the rights to issue sheet music by the blues legend, Robert Johnson.

August 1966 saw the surreal side of British industry; can you believe that the Philips pressing plant had an annual shutdown every summer irrespective of demand levels? This being so, Immediate had to go elsewhere to get promotional copies of The McCoys *(You Make Me Feel) So Good* pressed[15], which explains why the tiny number of promotional copies that have cropped up on the collectors' circuit over the last thirty or so years didn't look like Philips pressings.

At the tail end of 1966, Philips waxed lyrical in *Billboard* about its taking of 20% of the UK singles market during the year, helped by its pressing and distribution of independent labels, such as Immediate, Page One and Planet, all of which were name–checked[16]. However, a week later came the news that, following negotiations by Allen Klein, EMI had acquired distribution rights to Immediate product both in the UK and worldwide, excluding the US and Canada, where distribution rights were still being negotiated[17]. That said, Philips continued to press Immediate product well into the new year; all January and February releases being Philips pressings. The move seems, genuinely, to have seen goodwill remaining on both sides. The first EMI–pressed record was Twice As Much's *Crystal Ball*, which was issued in April 1967.

The move to EMI came about because the initial two year marketing agreement with Philips had expired and Oldham and Calder decided that EMI could do better in promoting Immediate product in Europe[18]. The deal was further commemorated by the introduction of a new company single sleeve design with the now famous, "Happy To Be A Part Of The Industry Of Human Happiness" slogan emblazoned across it.

Talking of single sleeves, there has been a great deal of discussion about the appearance of a handful of Philips–era sleeves with blue instead of black overprinting. If you compare one of these sleeves to the current Fontana single sleeves, you'll notice that the blue is the same. Either it was an accident or the printing plant ran out of black one day and didn't think it would matter too much to use the nearest colour. These are the most likely explanations, but that hasn't stopped some pointlessly wild speculation on this particular point.

In March 1967, Andrew Oldham and Tony Calder were back in the US looking for an outlet for Immediate product there. Until now, only one single had been released in the US, on MGM, and the sticking point seems to have been that both Oldham and Calder wanted a deal whereby Immediate product would be Immediate–branded rather than appearing on the US company's more usual label design.

> Andrew Oldham and Tony Calder...held talks in London, New York and Hollywood with executives of several major companies with a view to obtaining release for Immediate under its own logo in America...Apart from a one–shot deal with MGM Immediate product has not been issued in the U.S., as Oldham and Calder were anxious to establish their own identity in as many world markets as possible.[19]

MGM's halfway house approach was to include the Immediate logo, badly superimposed on the MGM label design, though not even this was done consistently and known one–off Immediate releases via MGM (Chris Farlowe's *Out Of Time* plus Twice As Much's *Sitting On A Fence* and *Step Out Of Line*) appear haphazardly both with and without this logo.

In March, *Billboard* announced that Immediate had signed the Small Faces, who would record for Immediate Productions with the tapes leased to Decca[20]. Oldham wasn't very happy with this arrangement and, according to Simon Spence, borrowed £25,000 from his Rolling Stones income to buy the Small Faces out of their current agreements with their manager, Don Arden, and Decca. Decca then pulled a fast one by issuing an album of demos and out–takes to coincide with the band's first album for Immediate – could it be that someone at Decca had learned some lessons from the Immediate book of sharp practice?

Talking of the Small Faces' LP, 1967 was a bit of a funny year on the LP front for Immediate. In the year of *Sgt Pepper*, when the pop LP seemed to come of age, Immediate released only this one rush–released LP.

Oldham kept his hand in on the production front and produced Marianne Faithfull for Decca release and Del Shannon for Liberty during March 1967 (though the subsequent Shannon LP was shelved by Liberty). The Small Faces also set up their own publishing company, Avakak, in conjunction with Immediate, and started their new lives as pop producers with Apostolic Intervention, another East End band[21].

Later the same month, *Billboard* stated that US negotiations with MGM were almost complete, whilst confirming the new UK pressing and distribution deal with EMI. Twice As Much were misnamed as Thrice As Much in one article[22]. There's inflation in action for you. The forthcoming 'deal' with MGM, as negotiated with Allen Klein[23], was not destined to last long and by July Immediate was also badgering EMI with its wish to have its own label imprint in Europe[24], rather than being bundled in with EMI's Stateside and Columbia artists.

As part of its thrust into Europe, a package tour, made up of the Small Faces, P.P. Arnold, Chris Farlowe and Twice As Much, was unleashed on Germany, Belgium, Luxembourg, France, Holland and Switzerland – all this in a week. Oldham flew into Bremen for the start of this tour from Los Angeles, where he had been helping to organise the Monterey Pop Festival. No sooner was the tour over than they all found themselves on a promotional visits to Finland, Sweden, Norway, Denmark, Spain and Italy – in Italy, the above four artists were joined by new signing, Nicky Scott. The itinerary, apart from live performance (presumably), included meeting disk jockeys, TV, radio and newspaper journalists, producers, pluggers and record company officials, plus giving radio interviews, attending receptions and filming for TV[25]. Who'd be a popular musician?

As regards market share, the majors were still in charge but, of the independents, Immediate came second to Phil Solomon's Major Minor label, with Island coming in third thanks to recent hits from Traffic. Overall the independents took 3.4% of market share. Decca, meanwhile, came out on top with EMI in second place[26].

Meanwhile, Immediate got involved in both films and books. The company had already created a promotional film under the direction of Peter Whitehead, titled *The Little Bastard Immediate*, and he became a partner in Immediate's book company. Oldham and Calder told *Record Mirror* (exact issue unknown) that they intended to publish five books by October 1967, one of which was to be a paperback. Immediate Publishing was really only a question of Immediate putting its name to the pre–existing Lorimer Publications, which Whitehead had set up as an outlet for screenplays.

In Simon Spence's *Immediate* book, Peter Whitehead has the following to say about Immediate's book publishing activities:

> When I started ... Lorimer Publications, we did screenplays, bought a load of rights off various film directors, did something on Che Guevara, made *Benefit Of The Doubt* with the Royal Shakespeare Company about Vietnam. Andrew distributed them and everything; he put up the money. For a year and a half they financed it all and it became Immediate Publishing. We even published some books together, all based on cinema. Then I took it back because somebody came along and offered me a better deal. I went back ... and said: 'Listen guys ... I wanna go off and do it as Lorimer again.' They said: 'Okay, whatever.'

In fact, Immediate had issued a book as early as 1966. The rear sleeve of several early LPs includes the following under the lurid command, "SPECIAL: ORDER NOW!"

> THE STARS OF IMMEDIATE RECORDS from the McCOYS to CHRIS FARLOWE and the low–down on the record business written by top show biz writers is available in a new book, THE IMMEDIATE RECORDS SUCCESS STORY. The book is completely free to you by sending a stamped addressed envelope to the address on the right–hand side.

Interesting to note is that the sleeve for the mono version of Mark Murphy's sole Immediate album. credits the book as "The Immediate Art Records Success Story", though this appears to be the only place to include the word "Art" in the title – the sleeve for the stereo version excludes it.

In September, Oldham appeared at an industry sales conference, where a 15 minute film about Immediate (filmed by Whitehead and titled *Here Come The Nice*, was shown and attendees were presented with a promotional booklet. Apart from this, there was a mixed bag for attendees:

> Guest speakers at the conference were CBS Sales manager Carl Denker, MGM Promotion Manager Peter Prince, Dr. Ronald Young of Delyse Records, and Frank Weintrop of Walt Disney Productions. Young addressed the delegates on the size and importance of the children's market, and Weintrop showed film clips including extracts from "Jungle Book" and "The Happiest Millionaire["] ... John Mew from EMI's Hayes office gave a talk on shop fitting. The conference concluded with a dinner at the Mount Royal Hotel, with cabaret entertainment featuring Ken Dodd and Alan Smethurst, the Singing Postman.[27]

The long–awaited news that Immediate had finally found a compatible US outlet, and one which included Canada, was announced on 23 September. A celebratory photograph in *Billboard* shows Tony Calder, looking somewhat glum, a bearded Andrew Oldham, looking close to violence, and a beaming Clive J. Davis, Vice President and General Manager of CBS. The Small Faces' *Itchycoo Park* was planned as the first release under the new deal[28], though it was December before the first LP, by the Small Faces, was issued[29]. It has to be said that it had a lovely sleeve design.

What wasn't mentioned was that, as documented by Simon Spence, Tony Calder had already signed an agreement with United Artists to distribute Immediate in the US – US copies of *Here Come The Nice* exist with United Artists credits – but Oldham refused to honour the deal. United Artists didn't take kindly to this and took Immediate to the cleaners, demanding $250,000 to void their contract and allow Immediate to move to CBS. The payments were staggered with the first $25,000 falling due in 1968, the next payment of $50,000 in 1969 and the final payment of $175,000 in 1970. A rider to the deal that caused a lot of pain was that if Immediate defaulted on the payment, then United Artists would get full rights to the Immediate Music publishing company.

In March 1968 there was news of some reshuffling within Immediate. Timothy Hardacre, previously the company's Legal Advisor, became a Director along with Andrew Oldham and Tony Calder, whilst ex–hairdresser, Ken Mew, previously Promotion Manager, became General Manager. Jim Watson, previously a Promoter for EMI, came in to run the Artists Department. This jiggery pokery in London coincided with Immediate opening offices in both Los Angeles and Sydney[30].

Later in the year, Immediate launched the Instant label and in November another new label, Revolution, was unveiled. Revolution was intended to focus on the soul and blue–beat markets and was launched on Friday 15 November 1968 as a subsidiary of Instant, rather than of Immediate (even if the first release stated "Immediate Records Limited" rather conspicuously on labels). Perhaps Instant's accounts showed a healthier balance than did Immediate's at this point. Only two singles were released before Immediate's involvement with Revolution came to an end.

Also in November, it was announced that Andrew Oldham was working on the musical score of an adaptation of *Gulliver's Travels*, which was to be directed by Sean Kenny and presented jointly by Oldham and Bernard Miles at the Mermaid Theatre. Long John Baldry was originally named as the lead[31], though by the time the production opened on 19 December, Mike d'Abo was in the title role.

By 1969, the lack of real movement in the US was starting to get Immediate down. Sales of Immediate product, after the good start with the Small Faces, was down to laughable numbers with various European–wide hits notching up total US sales of around a thousand, if they got as far as a US release, that is. Still, the original deal for two years with an option for a third year was just about to expire and it was expected that CBS would turn down the option for the third year.

On the artist front Immediate got Amen Corner, though they allowed both Chris Farlowe and P.P. Arnold to leave the label (both were signed by Polydor) along with the now Steve Marriott–less Small Faces (which, with the addition of Ron Wood and Rod Stewart, signed to Warner Brothers). Oldham and Calder had decided to run with Steve Marriott's new group instead. Amen Corner's first single for the label hit number one, which gave Immediate its second and last visit to the top of the UK singles chart. CBS, meanwhile, refused to release the Amen Corner single in the US. In April, *Billboard* described Scott Walker as an Immediate artist[32], though this was jumping the gun somewhat because the deal never quite materialised.

Simon Spence's Immediate book takes up the story based on a lack of information in contemporary trade publictaions. Oldham had been given the heads–up that he was going to have to pay a hefty tax bill on his Rolling Stones earnings and cost savings became the name of the game. In theory at least. Immediate moved from their New Oxford Street offices to 111, Gloucester Place, W.1. The next company into the vacated New Oxford Street offices was Warner Brothers so the Small Faces must have felt quite at home.

Problems reappeared in the US in July, 1969, however, when CBS insisted on taking up its option on distributing Immediate product for a third year. Oldham sued CBS claiming that the third year option had only been taken to suppress Immediate as a competitor in the US and Canada. Oldham then stated that Immediate was going independent in the US. On the one hand this cost a lot of money and, predictably, on the other hand CBS threatened legal action against the independent distributors. So the recent Nice LPs that Immediate had had pressed up couldn't be got to the shops.

CBS added insult to injury by pressing up the new Nice album as well, but then didn't bother to promote it. Unplayed, sealed copies still turn up for sale. Oldham, meanwhile, was not allowed within 100 yards of the CBS building because of threats made against CBS' head, Clive Davis. Tony Stratton Smith, the Nice's manager, used the chaos in the US to get the band out of their deal with Immediate and set up his own label, Charisma, for whom the next Nice album was a major hit.

It became fairly clear that Immediate would not be able to honour the final payment to United Artists and that the company was falling apart. There was some talk about a merger with Island, but this didn't materialise, and by Christmas 1969 Oldham and Calder had decided to shut up shop. Oldham bought out Calder with his Rolling Stones income and so, by the time of the creditors meeting, it was Oldham himself that was Immediate's largest creditor.

United Artists, meanwhile, got the rights to Immediate Music, as per the payment default agreement. One of the first benefits to United Artists was the Ten Years After track, *Goin' Home*, included on the Woodstock soundtrack, which was published by Immediate Music. The sort of money this earned United Artists might just have been enough to keep Immediate afloat a little longer. Immediate Music's Malcolm Forrester, what with finding his publishing company pulled out from under his feet, started his own publishing company, Gateway Music, which almost immediately picked up publishing rights for Juicy Lucy[33].

So, that was the end of Immediate Records Ltd., but in the US, Immediate Records Inc. was still a going concern. Was this going to cause confusion later on? You bet!

Although Immediate was decalared bankrupt in March 1970, the label lived on – literally. Fly Records used up the remaining Immediate 7" label blanks, which explains why T Rex's *Ride A White Swan* (BUG 1) appeared in 1970 on a familiar–looking lilac label and also why John Kongos' *He's Gonna Step On You Again* (BUG 8) in 1971 had a very familiar pink label. The discographer in me has to point out that all copies of BUG 1 seem to be solid centre copies whilst both solid and four–prong die–cut centres exist for BUG 8.

Post–Immediate

In music industry terms, almost every maverick–run record label owes its existence to Immediate. Immediate showed the way and showed that an independent record label could – up to a point – dictate its own terms and succeed. Charisma, Virgin, Stiff, Rough Trade, Cherry Red, Riot City, Factory, Pop God, Creation – would these labels have done what they did without Immediate's lead? In fact, would they have existed?

By the early 1970s various record labels were keen to exploit the Immediate archive based on the popularity of current superstars, such as Keith Emerson, Eric Clapton, Fleetwood Mac, Jimmy Page, The Faces and Humble Pie, not to mention the various Rolling Stones connections.

Andrew Oldham lived in the US for three years to avoid having to pay his Rolling Stones tax bill, allowable by certain failings in the then UK tax laws, and he and Dan Crewe's Andan Productions licensed much Immediate material, mostly in one–off deals:

> RCA Records next month will issue the first volume in a new British Blues Archives Series. More volumes will be issued later in the year. Tapes for the series were acquired from Immediate Records, a British label no longer in existence. Featured in the series will be such young pop blues artists as Eric Clapton, John Mayall, Jeff Beck, Jimmy Page, Nicky Hopkins and Jo–Ann Kelly.[34]

In 1971, James Q. Watson, who had worked for the Immediate Artists management company, moved from the UK to Canada to join Love Productions' Daffodil and Strawberry labels as product manager[35]. It should come as no surprise to discover that almost the first thing he did was reissue large chunks of Immediate back catalogue.

In 1972, artists signed to Andan Productions were distributed in the US by Motown on their Mowest label – November saw one LP each by Repairs and Kubie released via this arrangement. Earlier in 1972, negotiations had been finalised for A&M in the US to reissue a double–set of the first two Immediate Humble Pie LPs as *Lost and Found.* Oddly, an article about the Andan/Motown distribution deal stated, "…the current chart album "Lost and Found," contain[s] Humble Pie's first two albums for Immediate, their U.S.–based label which went into liquidation last year."[36] Subsequent action via Immediate Records Inc. would suggest that the article was most likely referring to the UK rather than US company with incorrect year stated. Probably.

In 1973, Daffodil issued seven further albums of Immediate back catalogue. These were issued via Capitol in Canada and in the US via Peters International, the New York–based specialist import company. The LPs – also available on cassette and 8–track – were: *The Gold Hits of Immediate*; P.P. Arnold's *Kafunta*; Duncan Brown's *Give Me Take You*; *The Art of Chris Farlowe*; The Nice's *The Thoughts of Emerlist Davjack*; *Small Faces*; and *Anthology of British Blues #3*[37].

Amusingly, Duncan Browne was described, in the above article as, "a British singer/songwriter who has never been off the English charts for long" whilst breaking news on the Nice front was that, "Brian [Davison] and Lee [Jackson] are rejoining to form a new edition of Nice." This, of course, was new band, Refugee. Meanwhile, the scarcity of copies on the collectors' scene suggests that sales of such delights as the Duncan Browne and P.P. Arnold albums were not particularly great.

By 1974, Oldham had set up yet another production company, Because Productions. The first release was by the 18–year old US singer, Brett Smiley, whose *Va–Va–Va–Voom* single was issued in the UK by Anchor Records, complete in picture sleeve, on Friday, 27 September[38]. Despite (or probably because of) Smiley's and Oldham's appearance on *The Russell Harty Show* on 20 September (where Smiley pouted and posed along to the self–penned b–side, *Space Age* and neither Smiley nor Oldham – or a peevish and self–righteous Harty for that matter – distinguished themselves during the subsequent interview) the record buying public stayed away in their hordes and the single bombed, which is a shame because it ain't that bad. The LP from which the single was taken was shelved and only appeared in 2004. It can be guessed from Oldham's appearance on UK TV that his tax–related exile was now over.

In the UK, nothing of an Immediate flavour reappeared – a re–licensing from the US Bang label of The McCoys' *Hang On Sloopy* LP on the Joys label and a one–off New World label budget compilation of potentially 'interesting' provenance excepted – until Tony Calder found himself back in the UK to run the Opal sub–label for the resurrected NEMS record label. The NEMS label had been dormant since putting out a spate of records in 1968 and 1969, and was owned by father and son team, Patrick and Patrick Meehan. Their latest venture had been World Wide Artists, or WWA, a management and record company that included Black Sabbath, The Groundhogs and Gentle Giant. WWA, however, didn't seem to survive beyond 1974 and NEMS appears to have been, to some extent, WWA metamorphosed with, perhaps tellingly, new manufacturer and distributor. Certainly, no new WWA product appeared after 1974, whilst NEMS, as a record label, reappeared during 1975 with Black Sabbath as its flagship artist.

With Calder on board, NEMS had grand plans to resurrect the Immediate label and to reissue selected material, starting with The Small Faces' *Itchycoo Park*. Not only was the group to reform to make a video, but NEMS had plans for a new Small Faces album as well, not that this latter event happened – at least, the group did later reform (minus Ronnie Lane) and released two disappointing albums for Atlantic. Perhaps they should have used a different name for the project. Humble Faces or Small Pie perhaps. Whether the group realised it or not, there was a great deal of expectation from a Small Faces reunion and two LPs of bland, mid–Atlantic rock 'n' soul didn't meet that expectation even half way.

Meanwhile, back in August 1975, the newly–formed Charly label seemed to pip NEMS to the post, when *Billboard* announced the label's intention to reissue choice cuts from the Immediate back catalogue:

> Musically historic back–product from the Sun, Red Bird and Immediate catalogs – all important forces in early rock music – will soon be available again via Charly Records, a newly–formed company in the U.K. headed by former EMI label a&r manager Joop Visser … Albums have already been scheduled by the Small Faces, Nice and Humble Pie. And an agreement between Oldham and Charly gives the new company rights to all new product from Oldham's Because Productions.[39]

Charly LPs, with music licensed from Immediate Records Inc. – Oldham's US company – appeared in the UK in 1975 and 1976. The ludicrous upshot of this was that *Ogden's Nut Gone Flake*, after being unavailable in the UK for five years was suddenly available from two UK record labels at the same time.

It is generally stated that NEMS bought Immediate from the liquidator in 1976, which if correct is *after* they'd already started to release Immediate back–catalogue, both the *Out Of Time* and *Itchycoo Park* NEMS reissues charted in 1975. The guess is that the deal had already been done in 1975. Probably. Or did the company think that employing Calder would legitimise releasing Immediate material? If this was the case, did anyone take into account that Calder had been bought out of Immediate by Oldham shortly before the company had collapsed? What, of course makes all of this so difficult to disentangle is that there were still the two distinct companies to worry over. The liquidated UK company and the US Immediate Inc. Although Calder had been bought out of the UK concern, it's anyone's guess as to whether he still retained ownership of any Immediate Inc. assets).

Back with the NEMS deal, according to Simon Spence's book, what they bought from the UK liquidator was Immediate's assets, such as the branding and the music, but not the company's liabilities, such as artist contracts, which meant that they didn't have to pay royalties. Meanwhile, Andrew Oldham was invited by his old partner, Tony Calder, to become something along the lines of 'director of special projects' or 'executuve catalyst' with NEMS for the Immediate project. The meeting took place at the Midem Music Festival in Cannes. Perhaps it was just bad luck that Oldham sailed to Cannes with Don Arden. Arden was Black Sabbath's manager and had some problems with the Meehans. The upshot was that Arden stuck a gun in Tony Calder's mouth at some point during the procedings. It then came to light that Calder was living with Oldham's ex–wife. Perhaps it's no surprise that a deal between Oldham and NEMS didn't come off.

Some sort of deal must have been made with Charly, because that company ceased to release any further Immediate material in the UK from 1976. That doesn't mean to say that it wasn't available in the UK throughout the late 1970s. Various *Music Master* trade publications list the Charly records as being available as French imports. The fact that many (if not all) of these French imports seem to have been UK pressings, presumably exported to France and re–imported to the UK in the meantime, is merely a curiosity.

Once the UK pressings had run out the UK market was inundated with cheap Italian imports on the Oxford label. And once the five year deal with Oldham was up, according to Simon Spence, Charly just carried on pressing the records up.

Meanwhile, that NEMS had, completely legally, got out of any responsibility as regards doing anything so mundane as paying royalties to the artists involved on future sales of back catalogue must have rankled somewhere and it came as a bit of a surprise when, in 1977, an accountancy firm contacted the *NME* for help in finding the whereabouts of artists that had been signed to Immediate so that outstanding royalty payments could be made. In a subsequent article, the *NME* had the following to say:

> ...an accountancy firm [sent a] letter to NME claiming the sale of the Immediate catalogue had now been completed and that outstanding royalty payments could be made to all Immediate artists...the lawyers confirmed that the entire catalogue has been bought by NEMS, the cash settlement allowing past royalties to be paid. Peter Knight of NEMS says all contracts have now been renegotiated, and there are plans to reintroduce Immediate product slowly but surely on to the market. Already out are The Small Faces "Ogden" album alongside two of their best singles, "Lazy Sunday" and "Itchycoo Park", Chris Farlowe's "Out Of Time" was a chart hit second time round and was backed by a "Best Of". . . album, while Amen Corner and Nice albums rounded off the first batch of releases. Plans for 1977 involve 12 albums and six singles including vinyl from Humble Pie and P.P. Arnold. And when the re–releases start wearing thin, there are also plans to introduce new talent to the label. So Immediate lives on![40]

As regards new talent, NEMS had signed Marianne Faithfull with the intention of releasing her new material on Immediate, though the subsequent records were issued instead on the NEMS label proper (though *Faithless* was issued on Immediate in Canada). The only 'new' material that appeared was an odd coupling of Crispian St. Peters' Decca hit, *You Were On My Mind* with a track credited to Traxtor, which seems to be the backing track for The Truth's Deram label cover of Donovan's *Hey Gyp (Dig The Slowness)* and a throw–away track on the b–side of a P.P. Arnold single credited to "The Immediate All Stars", conspicuous by being the only track issued on the Immediate–branded NEMS label not to be credited as "an original Immediate recording".

And so the late 1970s progressed with nothing much of note happening other than that NEMS changed manufacturer fairly regularly, which may or may not be significant, though it *tends* to suggest cash flow problems. In the early 1980s there seemed to be a lot of NEMS spin–off companies, which also may not be significant, although *this* looks a lot like spreading eggs around various baskets just in case one or other basket should be visited by the liquidator.

NEMS, meanwhile, dropped Calder at some point, unspecified, and, as from late 1982, NEMS records started to appear with the credit, "Issued under Licence to Pablocrown Ltd." and, later, "Issued under licence to Zeema Records Ltd". The question here is were Pablocrown Ltd. and Zeema Records Ltd. NEMS spin–offs or had (at least part of) NEMS been bought out? Certainly, Zeema was at one point located in the same London street (31, Kings Road) in which the original NEMS Artists Agency Ltd. had been based (1, Kings Road), but there again, SW3 was home to lots of music–related companies. (Zeema was later listed at 15/19, Cavendish Place, London, W1M 0DD.)

As for NEMS itself, again there is only partial information freely available. NEMS Artistes Agency Ltd. was incorporated 19, March 1974 and this was joined by NEMS Enterprises Ltd., which was incorporated 31, December 1978, and NEMS Management Ltd., which was incorporated 5, May 1982. NEMS Artistes Agency Ltd. was eventually struck off and dissolved from the companies register on 30, March 2003 following compulsary liquidations on 16, February 1987 and 17, February 1989.

Meanwhile, enter Castle Communications, incorporated in 1983, which quickly started to buy up various ailing record companies. According to Simon Spence, Castle bought NEMS in 1983 but this date is not certain; for example, The Small Faces' *The Autumn Stone* was reissued in 1984 via, according to *Music Master*, "Immediate/NEMS/Stage One" (it wasn't until the 1986 edition that a Castle–distributed reissue was confirmed). In fact, the first confirmed Immediate back catalogue material appeared on various issues in the *Castle Collector Series* in November 1985, at which point Immediate reissues got very difficult to follow, especially with the first CD release of Immediate material appearing amongst the cassette and LP versions in 1986 (or possibly late 1985, depending on who you believe). Luckily, for this discographer, at least, this takes us well outside the time–span covered by Immediate's first twenty years.

The last releases that concern this discography are various hit single tracks licensed to Old Gold in early 1985. By this time the licensing credit had changed again to, "Issued under licence from Interworld Communications (Records) Ltd." This may possibly have been a Castle spin–off company getting some quick income following the purchase of the Immediate back–catalogue but, again, this is not confirmed. What doesn't help is that there have been at least three companies incorporated as Interworld Communications Ltd. over the years; it is likely that this particular one was the one dissolved 4, May 1993, but there again it might not be.

If anyone fancies disentangling the next thirty or so years, including Oldham and Calder's next attempt at getting Immediate back off the ground in the US in 1994[40] (this time with back catalogue from Marianne Faithfull and The Yardbirds added), you have my most sincere best wishes. Just as long as it isn't me that has to do it.

Section sources and notes

1. No author attributed (21 August 1965) "International News Reports: Music Capitals of the World: UK Decca, Stones Pact; Minus US", Billboard, p 26.
2. No author attributed (28 August 1965) "International News Reports: Oldham Gets Exclusive U.K. Release Rights to Bang label", Billboard, p24 cont'd p 29.
3. Chris Hutchins (5 March 1966) "International News Reports: From The Music Capitals of the World: London", Billboard, p 37.
4. Andre de Vekey (4 September 1965) "International News Reports: Analysis: 3 Moves Seen Major Significance In Shaping U.K. Industry's Future", Billboard, p 18.

5. No author attributed (18 September 1965) "International News Reports: Music Capitals of the World: Immediate Hit For Immediate", Billboard, p 4.
6. No author attributed (9 October 1965) "Wexler Burns European Oil", Billboard, p 12.
7. Chris Hutchins (2 October 1965) "International News Reports: Music Capitals of the World: London", Billboard, p 24.
8. Chris Hutchins (30 October 1965) "International News Reports: Music Capitals of the World: London", Billboard, p 24.
9. Chris Hutchins (1 January 1966) "Jolly Good '66 Seen for U.K.", Billboard, p 1 cont'd p 20 (the continued article on p. 20 had the title changed to "A Jolly 1966 Seen for U.K.").
10. Chris Hutchins (5 February 1966) "International News Reports: Immediate Weighs Bids for U.S. Outlet", Billboard, p 26.
11. No author attributed (23 April 1966) "Stones & Oldham Reacquire Firm", Billboard, p 6.
12. No author attributed (13 August 1966) "International News Reports: British Indies Show Strength on Pop Charts; 'Out of Time' No 1", Billboard, p 63.
13. Don Wedge (20 August 1966) International "News Reports: From The Music Capitals of the World: London", Billboard, p 55.
14. Ibid.
15. Ibid.
16. No author attributed (17 December 1966) "International News Reports: High Riding Philips Ready, Willing And Able to Do Peak Business in '67", Billboard, p 53.
17. No author attributed (24 December 1966) "Immediate Distrib Rights Go to EMI", Billboard, p 37.
18. No author attributed (11 March 1967) "Oldham and Calder Seek Deals For Release of Immediate label", Billboard, p 3.
19. Ibid.
20. Ibid.
21. Ibid.
22. Graeme Andrews (25 March 1967) "International News Reports: From The Music Capitals of the World: London", Billboard, p 54.
23. No author attributed (16 July 1967) "International News Reports: From The Music Capitals of the World: Immediate and MGM in Deal", Billboard, p 52.
24. No author attributed (15 July 1967) "International News Reports: From The Music Capitals of the World: Immediate Opens Major On the European Market", Billboard, p 7.
25. Ibid.
26. No author attributed (29 July 1967) "International News Reports: British Decca Topples EMI as Chart Leaders in England", Billboard, pp 46–48.
27. Nigel Hunter (16 September 1967) "International News Reports: EMI Bows High–Flying Plans On Int'l Front at Sales Meet", Billboard, p 68.
28. No author attributed (23 September 1967) "CBS to Distribute Immediate in U.S. in 2d Outside Label Deal", Billboard, p 3.
29. No author attributed (9 December 1967) Untitled Immediate trade advertisement", Billboard, p 1.
30. Nigel Hunter (9 March 1968) "International News Reports: From The Music Capitals of the World: London", Billboard, p 45.
31. Philip Palmer (9 November 1968) "International News Reports: From The Music Capitals of the World: London", Billboard, p 62.
32. Philip Palmer (12 April 1969) International News Reports: London, Billboard, p 65.
33. No author attributed (13 June 1970) International News Reports: London, Juicy Lucy, Immediate Tie, Billboard, p 65.
34. No author attributed (19 September 1970) "General News: British Blues Pkg on RCA", Billboard, p 3.
35. No author attributed (11 December 1971) "International News Reports: From The Music Capitals of the World: Canada Executive Turntable", Billboard, p 55.
36. No author attributed (11 November 1972) "General News: Andan, Motown Pact Renewed", Billboard, p 8.
37. No author attributed (24 November 1973) "Canadian News: Capitol Canada: Immediate Series On Daffodil", Billboard, p 51.
38. No author attributed (28 September 1974) "International: From The Music Capitals of the World: London", Billboard, p T65 (special trade section).
39. No author attributed (9 August 1975) "International: Charly Records To Issue Sun, Red Bird, Immediate ' Oldies'", Billboard, p 64.
40. John May (9 April 1977) “Read This – There’s Money In It!, New Musical Express, page unknown.
41. No author attributed (9 April 1994) "International: In The Fast Lane", Billboard, p 38.

SOURCE INFORMATION

Sources used in lists

[1] *The New Records* (monthly publication)
[2] *New Cassettes & Cartridges* (monthly publication)
[3] *The New Singles* (weekly publication)
[4] *Music Master* (2nd edition, 1976)
[5] *Music Master* (5th edition, 1979)
[6] *Music Master* (10th Edition, 1984)
[7] *Music Master* (11th Edition, 1985)
[8] *Music Master British Pop Singles 1975–84: Title Index* (1985)
[9] *Music Master Labels List '89* (9th Edition, 1989)
[10] *Demo/promo label*
[11] *Press release*
[12] *Music press advertisment* (source publication specified in listing)
[13] *Record Collector* (Issue 250, June 2000)
[14] *EMI Records Export Numerical Catalogue Service* (EMI in–house publication, January 1970)

The first three trade publications above were published by Francis Antony, whilst the *Music Master* series was published by John Humphries. Each source is represented in the listings by superscript numbers: e.g. [1] next to a list item means that the information was sourced from *The New Records*, whilst the month listed indicates the exact edition.

Release and deletion dates

For all items still on catalogue as at January 1970, release dates have been sourced from the EMI Records *Export Numerical Catalogue Service* listings for Immediate and Instant. These are accurate for all EMI–era releases, though many (but not all) Philips–era releases seem to have been rounded up with an arbitrarily–assigned (incorrect) release date.

Dates sourced from *The New Records* and *The New Cassettes and Cartridges* often tend to be a month out because both were issued mid–month. For example, an April release notified in March would miss the April edition if that issue had already gone to print. The listing, therefore, would appear in the May edition, itself issued mid–April. Wherever there is a discrepency in release date, all conflicting sources are listed.

Where a date exists in the singles and EP listings but no source is indicated, then release date is as taken from the record label if year only, or from *45cat.com* if there is mention of date and/or month. In these instances dates have not been independently verified. Also, release dates for one or two LPs sourced from *Record Collector* issue 250 could not be otherwise independently verified, though the dates in all these cases appear to be eminently believable!

Deletion dates are taken from *Music Master 2nd Edition*, which includes dates for LP deletions advised between 1973 and the end of 1975, *Music Master 5th Edition*, which includes all deletions advised up to the end of 1978 and *Music Master 11th Edition*, which includes all deletions advised up to the end of 1984. Note that deletion dates included in *Music Master Labels List '89* have a slightly suspicious look in that month of deletion for 1960s releases tends to match month of release. I would take the month of deletion with a pinch of salt if this represents the only source of deletion information.

Things get very confused with NEMS releases, especially in the 1980s, where records seem to have been re–repromoted several times through different distribution routes (some appearing in formats in which they'd not been issued on original release), each with more and more enigmatic licensing credits.

Original Immediate tape issues

The *EMI Records Export Numerical Catalogue Service* listings show the availability of tape versions (cassette, reel–to–reel and 8–track) of five Immediate LPs. However, none have surfaced on the collectors' market. The release date for all tapes is listed as December 1969, at which point Immediate was in the throes of bankruptcy. It is, therefore, possible that the only place that these tape versions exist is on paper. Tape versions are listed in the discography, based on the fact that they are documented as being available, even if none were subsequently manufactured. If anyone knows for sure, I'd like to know!

Recommended retail price

Prices for LPs and tapes are sourced from *The New Records*, *The New Cassettes and Cartridges* and the *Music Master* publications. Generally, the prices shown in *The New Records* and *The New Cassettes and Cartridges* are correct and so these are used as the main source. *Music Master* prices are shown where no other price source was available or where the price differs from that shown in *The New Records* and so on.

Organisation of the following label sections

Labels are listed in the order in which they first released Immediate–related records. Therefore, the listings begin, as you would expect, with Immediate (first release 1965) and finish with Old Gold (first Immediate–related release 1985).

Catalogue number sequences are listed in the order in which the first record in that sequence was released; e.g. Immediate's 7" IM 000 series singles come first, followed by 7" EPs, main sequence LPs, IMLYIN budget LPs and, finally, IMAL double LPs. Promotional–only records are rounded up at the end of label section irrespective of when records appeared.

The only exception to the above is that all re–releases of Immediate–era McCoys material on other labels has been rolled together into one section so as to prevent the inclusion of three otherwise scantily–filled pages. All of these are listed along with the first post–Immediate McCoys record release.

Note that two records are not documented amongst the reissue listings. The Nice's *Autumn '67 to Spring '68*, issued in 1972 by Charisma (and reissued by Pickwick), is made up of alternative recordings that were not originally issued by Immediate, whilst Chris Farlowe's Regal label LP was an export–only UK pressing, issued whilst Farlowe was still an Immediate artist. Both LPs are discussed instead within the Immediate listings.

IMMEDIATE

Immediate is surprisingly simple to document in terms of label designs with only two designs, each with a couple of variations, to worry over, as documented below:

- Lilac: the colour as used on both singles and LPs until November 1968
- Pink: the colour as used on both singles and LPs from November 1968

For lilac labels there are those with Philips marketing credits and those (mostly, but not all, EMI–era releases) without. First press of IM 001 to 003 did not include "Record Co. Ltd." under the Immediate logo. Most pink labels have "Sold in the UK..." text, though late 1969 pressings do not because of the removal of the Retail Price Index as related to the sale of records. Pink labels also became noticably lighter in late 1969, on LPs at least.

IM sequence 7" singles

Philips–era singles (August 1965 to February 1967) have three–pronged, die–cut centres, some also pressed with solid centres (early singles have a near–white label colour). EMI singles (April 1967 onward) have four–pronged, die–cut centres (many also pressed with solid centres). Promotional copies included "Demonstration Sample" text (all in upper case) and a large, red "A" – most also included the intended realease date. These are not documented in the following listing unless there is some deviation to the above.

The printed company sleeve design only changed once, that when manufacturing and distribution switched from Philips to EMI; the Philips ones mention "Philips" whilst the EMI ones don't. The only variation is that some early sleeves were overprinted in blue instead of black, and these seem to have accompanied copies of IM 001. Mine had a Rak label Julie Felix single inside, so I can't verify this, but enough people seem to agree!

IM 001 THE McCOYS: Hang On Sloopy/I Can't Explain It
Rel: 20 Aug 1965[11]/Sep 1966[14] **Del:** 1968[9]
Initial press excludes "Record Co. Ltd." under the logo. Philips–pressed solid centre copies exist. This remained on catalogue long enough for EMI pressed four–prong die–cut copies to be issued. Most Philips and all EMI pressings have Campbell Connelly, Robert Mellin and MCPS publishing credits on a–side. Some Philips copies credit Campbell Connelly only. Some early copies in blue overprinted company sleeves. The September 1966 release date on this and subsequent Philips–era singles represents an EMI round–up of pre–EMI releases with arbitrarily–assigned (incorrect) release date[14]. Number 5 in the UK charts (not number 1 as later claimed by Andrew Oldham).

IM 002 THE FIFTH AVENUE: The Bells Of Rhymney/Just Like Anyone Would Do
Rel: 20 Aug 1965[11]

IM 003 NICO: I'm Not Sayin/The Last Mile
Rel: 20 Aug 1965[11]/Sep 1966[14]
No apostrophe in title. Blank Immediate label copies with handwritten credits exist.

IM 004 GREGORY PHILLIPS: Down In The Boondocks/That's The One
Rel: 27 Aug 1965

IM 005 THE MASTERMINDS: She Belongs To Me/Taken My Love
Rel: 3 Sep 1965

IM 006 THE POETS: Call Again/Some Things I Can't Forget
Rel: 14 Oct 1965

IM 007 THE STRANGELOVES: Cara–Lin/(Roll On) Mississippi
Rel: 15 Oct 1965/Sep 1966[14]
On catalogue long enough to appear on the pink label design (four–prong, die–cut and solid–centre pink label copies confirmed). Licensed from Bang Records in New York though no logo on labels.

IM 008 VAN LENTON: Gotta Get Away/You Don't Care
Rel: 1 Oct 1965

IM 009 THE FACTOTUMS: In My Lonely Room/A Run In The Green and Tangerine Flaked Forest
Rel: 1 Oct 1965

IM 010 THE GOLDEN APPLES OF THE SUN: The Monkey Time/Chocolate Rolls, Tea And Monopoly
Rel: 22 Oct. 1965[11]
According to 45cat.com, Decca test pressings with matrix number XDR 36117/8 exist.

IM 011 BARBARA LYNN: You Can't Buy My Love/That's What A Friend Will Do
Rel: 29 Oct 1965

IM 012 JOHN MAYALL AND THE BLUESBREAKERS: I'm Your Witchdoctor/ Telephone Blues
Rel: 22 Oct 1965[11]
John Mayall gets top billing on the labels with "and the BLUESBREAKERS" printed in smaller point size. Later reissued as IM 051 with updated credit to cash in on Eric Clapton's increased popularity.

IM 013 GLYN JOHNS: Mary Anne/Like Grains Of Yellow Sand
Rel: 11 Nov 1965

IM 014 MICK SOFTLEY: I'm So Confused/She's My Girl
Rel: 25 Nov 1965

IM 015 THE MOCKINGBIRDS: You Stole My Love/Skit Skat
Rel: 8 Oct 1965
Beware 2005 reproduction copies with large centre hole.

IM 016 CHRIS FARLOWE: The Fool/Treat Her Good
Rel: 8 Oct 1965[11]
Promotional posters credited the single to "Chris Farlowe and the Thunderbirds" though the record labels credit Farlowe only. At least one blank Immediate label copy with handwritten credits exist.

IM 017 JOEY VINE: Down And Out/The Out Of Towner
Rel: 28 Oct 1965

IM 018 JIMMY TARBUCK: Someday/Wastin' Time
Rel: 14 Oct 1965

IM 019 THE VARIATIONS: The Man With All The Toys/She'll Know I'm Sorry
Rel: 3 Dec 1965
The labels also credit "INSTANT RECORDS N.Y."

IM 020 LES FLEURS DE LYS: Moondreams/Wait For Me
Rel: 7 Nov 1965

IM 021 THE McCOYS: Fever/Sorrow
Rel: 25 Nov 1965 **Del:** 1968[9]
Bang Records logo on labels. Number 44 in the UK charts.

IM 022 THE FACTOTUMS: You're So Good To Me/Can't Go Home Anymore My Love
Rel: 21 Jan 1966[10]

IM 023 CHRIS FARLOWE: Think/Don't Just Look At Me
Rel: 14 Jan 1966[10]/Sep 1966[14] **Del:** 1969[9]
Copies also confirmed with solid centres. Number 37 in the UK charts, probably helped by his recent performance on *Ready Steady Go* with Otis Redding and Eric Burdon.

IM 024 THE POETS: Baby Don't You Do It/I'll Come Home
Rel: 28 Jan 1966

IM 025 CHARLES DICKENS: So Much In Love/Our Soul Brother
Rel: 11 Feb 1966[10]

IM 026 GOLDIE: Going Back/Headlines
Rel: 4 Feb 1966
Demo labels do not include release date.

IM 027 TONY RIVERS AND THE CASTAWAYS: Girl Don't Tell Me/The Girl From Salt Lake City
Rel: 18 Feb 1966

IM 028 THE McCOYS: Don't Worry Mother, Your Son's Heart Is Pure/Ko–Ko
Rel: 21 Feb 1966/Oct 1966[14]
Bang Records logo on labels. EMI listings[14] include a one–off arbitrary release date (see IM 001)!

IM 029 THE McCOYS: Up And Down/If You Tell A Lie
Rel: 25 Feb 1966[10]/Sep 1966[14]
Bang Records logo on labels.

IM 030 THE LONDON WAITS: Softly Softly (The Theme From The BBC–TV Series)/Seranado (Italian Serenade)
Rel: 18 Mar 1966/Sep 1966[14]

IM 031 THE TURTLES: You Baby/Wanderin' Kind
Rel: 25 Mar 1966[10]/Sep 1966[14]
Includes "WHITE WHALE RECORD CO." credit on labels. Also incorrectly listed as IM 033[14].

IM 032 THE FLEUR DE LYS: Circles/So, Come On
Rel: 18 Mar 1966[10]
Artist credit changed from "Les Fleur De Lys" to "The Fleur De Lys" by the time of this single. Beware 2005 reproduction copies with large centre hole.

IM 033 TWICE AS MUCH: Sittin' On A Fence/Baby I Want You
Rel: 27 May 1966 **Del:** 1969[9]
Number 25 in the UK charts. Demo copy on Emidisc acetate exists credited to "David & Andrew".

IM 034 THE McCOYS: Runaway/Come On Let's Go
Rel: 3 Jun 1966[10]/Sep 1966[14]
Bang Records logo on labels.

IM 035 CHRIS FARLOWE: Out Of Time/Baby Make It Soon
Rel: 17 Jun 1966/Sep 1966[14] **Del:** 1969[9]
Also exists with solid centre with Philips credits. Four–prong die–cut copies also exist with Philips credits. The most likely explanation is that Philips contracted pressing to EMI to keep up with demand. Number 1 in the UK charts. Emidisc acetates with typewritten credits exist.

IM 036 TWICE AS MUCH: Step Out Of Line/Simplified
Rel: 19 Aug 1966/Sep 1966[14]
An Emidisc acetate exists with typewritten credits "I STEP OUT OF LINE"/"I STEP OUT OF LINE PART II" with the "I" crossed out on side 1 only. In felt tip pen on side 1, "FOR USE ON RSG ON AUG 19TH!" has been hand written with the initials "T.C." added, which presumably means that Tony Calder wrote this message relating to *Ready Steady Go*. Side 2 has the handwritten message, "THIS SIDE IS FOR ALO'S FRIENDS ONLY".

IM 037 THE McCOYS: (You Make Me Feel) So Good/Every Day I Have To Cry
Rel: 12 Aug 1966/Sep 1966[14]
Bang Records logo on labels. Title is printed as "(You make me feel) SO GOOD" on label.

IM 038 CHRIS FARLOWE: Ride On Baby/Headlines
Rel: 27 Oct 1966/Sep 1966[14] **Del:** 1969[9]
From this release onwards the Philips manufacturing and distribution credit was discontinued, though records were still manufactured by Philips. Also exists as a Philips pressing with solid centre. Number 31 in the UK charts.

IM 039 TWICE AS MUCH: True Story/You're So Good For Me
Rel: 18 Nov 1966/Sep 1966[14]
Demo copies include Philips marketing credits although stock copies do not and, unusually, demo label does not include release date.

IM 040 P. P. ARNOLD: Everything's Gonna Be Alright/Life Is But Nothing
Rel: 3 Feb[10]/Feb 1967[14]
Demo copies include Philips marketing credits although stock copies do not.

IM 041 CHRIS FARLOWE: My Way Of Giving/You're So Good for Me
Rel: Jan 1967[14] **Del:** 1969[9]
Number 48 in the UK charts.

The above single, along with IM 045 and IM 046, which were issued out of sequence, was the last to be manufactured by Philips and all further singles were either four–prong, die–cut or solid–centred EMI pressings.

IM 042 TWICE AS MUCH: Crystal Ball/Why Can't They All Go And Leave Me Alone
Rel: Mar[14]/7 Apr 1967[3]
Only solid–centred copies confirmed.

IM 043 THE APOSTOLIC INTERVENTION: (Tell Me) Have You Ever Seen Me/ Madame Garcia
Rel: Feb[14]/7 Apr 1967[3]

IM 044 NICKY SCOTT: Big City/Everything's Gonna Be Alright
Rel: Mar[14]/14 Apr 1967

IM 045 NICKY SCOTT: Backstreet Girl/Chain Reaction
Rel: Jan[14]/20 Jan 1967
Labels did not include Philips marketing credit although still manufactured by Philips.

IM 046 THE McCOYS: I Got To Go Back/Dynamite
Rel: Jan[14]/13 Jan 1967[10]
Philips–manufactured record. Bang Records logo on labels. Philips marketing credit on labels.

IM 047 P. P. ARNOLD: The First Cut Is The Deepest/Speak To Me
Rel: Apr[14]/28 Apr 1967[3]
Solid–centred copies also exist. No. 18 in UK charts. Demo version does not include release date.

IM 048 MORT SHUMAN IV: Monday Monday/Little Children
Rel: Apr[14]/21 Apr 1967[10]
This single does not seem to be listed in contemporary trade publications, though it was reviewed in the music press (e.g. NME, dated 29 April 1967). Stock copies exist, though most copies that crop up for sale seem to be demo copies, which would tend to suggest that sales were not great.

IM 049 CHRIS FARLOWE: Yesterday's Papers/Life Is But Nothing
Rel: Apr[14]/28 Apr 1967[3]
Only solid–centred copies confirmed.

IM 050 SMALL FACES: Here Come The Nice/Talk To You
Rel: Jun[14]/9 Jun 1967[3] **Del:** Jun 1970[9]
Solid–centred copies also exist. Number 12 in the UK charts.

IM 051 JOHN MAYALL AND THE BLUESBREAKERS WITH ERIC CLAPTON: I'm Your Witchdoctor/Telephone Blues
Rel: Jun[14]/9 Sep 1967[10]
Previously issued as IM 012, but now reissued with updated artist credit to make clear that the record includes Eric Clapton. John Mayall still gets the major billing with the Bluesbreakers and Eric Clapton credits in smaller point size.

IM 052 MARQUIS OF KENSINGTON: The Changing Of The Guard/MARQUIS OF KENSINGTON'S MINSTRELS: Reverse Thrust
Rel: May[14]/9 Jun 1967[3]
The title on the a–side is in ornate type face: the b–side title text is in the usual type face.

IM 053 MURRAY HEAD: She Was Perfection/Secondhand Monday
Rel: May[14]/26 May 1967[10]

IM 054 AUSTRALIAN PLAYBOYS: Black Sheep R.I.P./Sad
Rel: Jun[14]/16 Jun 1967[10]
Beware bootleg copies on the demo label design manufactured in 2000 with large centre hole.

IM 055 P. P. ARNOLD: The Time Has Come/If You See What I Mean
Rel: Jun[14]/30 Jun[10]/7 Jul 1967[3] **Del:** Aug 1972[9]
Number 47 in the UK charts.

IM 056 CHRIS FARLOWE: Moanin'/What Have I Been Doing
Rel: Jun[14]/23 Jun 1967[3] **Del:** 1969[9]
Only solid–centred copies confirmed. Number 46 in the UK charts.

IM 057 SMALL FACES: Itchycoo Park/I'm Only Dreaming
Rel: Jun[14]/11 Aug 1967[3] **Del:** Aug 1970[9]
Solid–centred copies are more numerous than the die–cut version. Number 3 in the UK charts.

IM 058 WARM SOUNDS: Sticks And Stones/Angeline
Rel: Jul[14]/28 Jul[10]/11 Aug 1967[3]

IM 059 THE NICE: The Thoughts Of Emerlist Davjack/Azrial Angel Of Death
Rel: Nov[14]/3 Nov[10]/10 Nov 1967[3]
"Angel of Death" appears is smaller point size, suggesting that this is a subtitle.

IM 060 ROD STEWART: Little Miss Understood/So Much To Say
Rel: Apr[14]/22 May 1968[10/3]

IM 061 P. P. ARNOLD: (If You Think) You're Groovy/Though It Hurts Me Badly
Rel: Jan[14]/5 Jan 1968[3] **Del:** 1971[9]
A rough mix of this song exists with blank Immediate labels and typewritten credit "Do You Think You're Groovy" (i.e. no brackets in the title). Number 41 in the UK charts.

IM 062 SMALL FACES: Tin Soldier/I Feel Much Better
Rel: 1 Dec[9]/15 Dec 1967[3] **Del:** Dec 1970[9]
Solid–centred copies also exist. This is the only original Immediate single to be released in picture sleeve in the UK. Number 9 in the UK charts.

IM 063 BILLY NICHOLLS: Would You Believe/Daytime Girl
Rel: 12 Jan 1968[10/3]

IM 064 SMALL FACES: Lazy Sunday/Rollin' Over (Part II Of Happiness Stan)
Rel: Apr[14]/5 Apr 1968[11/3]
Solid–centred copies also exist. "(Part II of Happiness Stan)" appears as a subtitle in smaller point size than the main track credit on both die–cut and solid centred copies. Later four–prong die–cut copies miss out "(Part II of Happiness Stan)". An Immediate labelled acetate exists with typewritten credits, including release date "5/4/68". Number 2 in the UK charts.

IM 065 CHRIS FARLOWE: Handbags And Gladrags/Everyone Makes A Mistake
Rel: Nov[14]/24 Nov 1967[3] **Del:** 1969[9]
Solid–centred copies also exist. Curiously, both four–pronged and solid–centered demo copies exist (all other EMI–era demos seem to be four–prong copies). The solid–centred version includes the "Sold in the UK..." text, which otherwise only appears on stock copies. The four–pronged demo, curiously, has "IM 065A" on both sides. An acetate exists with "1st mix" handwritten on the label. Number 33 in the UK charts.

IM 066 CHRIS FARLOWE: The Last Goodbye/CHRIS FARLOWE AND THE THUNDERBIRDS: Paperman Fly In The Sky

Rel: Apr[14]/12 Apr 1968[10]

A–side includes the subcredit, "(From the film "The Last Goodbye")".

IM 067 OUTER LIMITS: Great Train Robbery/Sweet Freedom (DEMOS ONLY)

IM 067 P. P. ARNOLD: Angel Of The Morning/Life Is But Nothing

Rel: Jun[14]/21 Jun 1968[3]

The Outer Limits single was not released though demos with a 10 May 1968 release date exist. A different version was issued instead on Instant, as IN 001, in September 1968. Catalogue number reassigned to P.P. Arnold's *Angel Of The Morning*, which was on catalogue long enough to appear on pink label. Both four–prong, die–cut and solid centred copies exist on the pink label.

IM 068 THE NICE: America (2nd Amendment)/Diamond Hard Blue Apples Of The Moon

Rel: Jun[14]/21 Jun 1968[3]

Solid–centred copies also exist. "(2nd Amendment)" appears as a subtitle in smaller point size than the main track credit. The label also includes the text, "AMERICA, Adapted From "West Side Story"". On catalogue long enough to appear on the pink label design. The pink label issue had amended credit, "America (from West Side Story)" with bracketed part in smaller point size than main track credit: "2nd Amendment" appears under the composer credit. Both four–prong, die–cut and solid–centred pink label copies exist; the b–side on both variations is credited as, "Diamond Hard Apples of the Moon" – i.e. missing out "Blue". The track timing of "7 min. 20 secs.", as mentioned in the original advert for the single, is incorrect. The correct track timing is around 6 mins. 25 secs. Andrew Loog Oldham wanted it to look as though it was longer than *Hey Jude*, at that point the longest single to chart in the UK. Number 16 in the UK charts.

IM 069 SMALL FACES: The Universal/Donkey Rides, A Penny A Glass

Rel: Jun[14]/29 Jun 1968 **Del:** Jul 1971[9]

On catalogue long enough to also appear on the pink label design. Copies exist with EMI Promotion Sample labels and handwritten credits.

IM 070 DUNCAN BROWNE: On The Bombsite/Alfred Bell

Rel: Jul[14]/12 Jul[11]/18 Jul 1968[3]

Both labels include the subcredit, "(from the album "Give Me Take You" IMSP018)". A box of 20 or so unplayed copies was unearthed from somewhere or other around 1980 and mint copies popped up for sale every now and then until the mid–1980s. A rough ("ruf") mix of the a–side, minus strings, exists on an Emidisc acetate (issued as a bonus track on the Sequel CD, CMRCD 057).

IM 071 CHRIS FARLOWE: Paint It Black/I Just Need Your Loving

Rel: Jul[14]/25 Jul 1968[3]

Includes the subcredit, "From the Album The Best of Chris Farlowe IMCP 010".

The above single was the last to be released on the lilac label design and all further releases were on the pink label design.

IM 072 THE NICE: Brandenburger/Happy Freuds

Rel: Nov[14]/15 Nov 1968[3]

Includes subcredit, "(From the album Ars Longa Vita Brevis IMSP 020)". A–side is edited from "3rd Movement Acceptance "BRANDENBURGER"" from the sidelong LP track, "Ars Longa Vita Brevis". This jazzed–up piece of Bach is credited to "Jackson, Emerson, Davison" on the label. Hm.

IM 073 AMEN CORNER: (If Paradise Is) Half As Nice/Hey Hey Girl

Rel: Jan[14]/17 Jan[10]/29 Jan[9]/31 Jan 1969[3]

Solid centre copies also exist. "(If Paradise Is)" appears in smaller point size than the rest of the track credit. Number 1 in the UK charts.

IM 074 CHRIS FARLOWE AND THE THUNDERBIRDS: Dawn/April Was The Month

Rel: Nov 1968[14]/3 Jan 1969[3]

IM 075 MICHAEL D'ABO: (See The Little People) Gulliver's Travels/An Anthology Of Gulliver's Travels – Part 2

Rel: 7 Feb[10]/14 Feb 1969[3]

"(See the Little People)" appears in smaller point size than the rest of the track credit. A further subcredit under the composer credit says, "(From the show Gulliver's Travels)". Withdrawn before release, according to an article in the *NME* ("D'Abo 'Little People' row", 19 Feb. 1969), though stock copies had already been pressed. The *NME* article goes on to say:

> ...D'Abo issued an injunction against Immediate to restrain that company from releasing the disc, and this was granted last Thursday. A spokesman for D'Abo told the NME; "All members of the Manfred Mann group, including Michael, are under exclusive contract to Fontana. When he recorded this number for Immediate, he was under the impression that permission had been obtained from Fontana, but such was not the case – and he was therefore obliged to take action." Also withdrawn – for similar reasons – is a "Gulliver's Travels" album.

IM 076 THE McCOYS: Hang On Sloopy/This Is Where We Came In

Rel: Feb[14]/7 Mar[3]/28 Mar 1969[10]

Includes "Bang Records N.Y." credit but does not include the bang logo on the labels.

IM 077 SMALL FACES: Afterglow Of Your Love/Wham Bam Thank You Man

Rel: Mar[14]/7 Mar 1969[10] **Del:** Mar 1972[9]

Solid centre copies also exist. Double a–side. This version of "Afterglow of Your Love" misses out the acoustic intro, but continues after the drum fill where other versions fade out. Emidisc acetates exist of the early version of *Wham Bam Thank You Man* titled as *Me, You and Us Too*. Demo version (IM 077 1F–1 matrix) plays *Me, You And Us Too*; stock copies have IM 077 2F–2 matrix. Number 36 in the UK charts. Although listed as deleted in 1972 two new copies turned up in mint company sleeves at *Rival Records*, Park Street, Bristol, in October 1981 (at 35p each). Guess who bought them!

IM 078 CHRIS FARLOWE: Out Of Time/Ride On Baby

Rel: Mar[14]/14 Mar 1969

IM 079 P. P. ARNOLD: The First Cut Is The Deepest/The Time Has Come

Rel: Mar[14]/21 Mar[10]/28 Mar 1969[3]

IM 080 FLEETWOOD MAC: Man Of The World/EARL VINCE AND THE VALIANTS: Somebody's Gonna Get Their Head Kicked In Tonite

Rel: Apr[14]/3 Apr[10]/11 Apr 1969[3] **Del:** Apr 1972[9]

Number 2 in the UK charts.

IM 081 AMEN CORNER: Hello Suzie/Evil Man's Gonna Win

Rel: Jun[14]/13 Jun 1969[10]/25 Jun 1969[9]

Solid centre copies also exist. Later four–prong, die–cut centred copies exist without "Sold in U.K." text. An Emidisc acetate exists with typewritten "Hello Suzie", but no artist credit. The exact issue of *The New Singles* is missing from the British Library collection, but it is included in the release round–up in the 27 June issue, meaning that it was either listed in the edition for 13 or 20 June.

IM 082 HUMBLE PIE: Natural Born Bugie/Wrist Job

Rel: Aug[14]/8 Aug[10]/15 Aug 1969[3] **Del:** 1972[9]

Solid centre copies also exist. Neither version includes "Sold in U.K." text.

IM 083 NOT RELEASED

Various theories exist and contenders include: P.P. Arnold's *Would You Believe / Am I Still Dreaming*, issued in March 1969 in Germany; Humble Pie's *The Sad Bag Of Shaky Jake / Cold Lady*, issued in various non–UK territories; The Nice's *Hang On To A Dream / Diary Of An Empty Day*, issued in Germany; and The Hill's *Sylvie / The Fourth Annual Convention Of The Battery Hen Farmers Association (Part II)*, issued in north America in June 1969. Perhaps it was something else altogether!

IM 084 AMEN CORNER: Get Back/Farewell To The Real Magnificent Seven

Rel: Oct[14]/17 Oct[10]/31 Oct 1969[3]

Labels do not include "Sold in U.K." text. Demo copies are on the usual demo label design but without "DEMONSTRATION SAMPLE" text. Trident acetates exist with handwritten credits.

IMEP sequence 7" EPs

IMEP 001 CHRIS FARLOWE: Farlowe in the Midnight Hour

1. In The Midnight Hour
2. Mr. Pitiful

1. Satisfaction
2. Who Can I Turn To

Rel: Nov 1965

Picture sleeve. The credits above are as printed on the tri–centre labels. The sleeve, however, includes a question mark at the end of the final track and "Satisfaction" is credited as "I can't get no SATISFACTION". Final track subcredited on sleeve with "from THE ROAR OF THE GREASEPAINT". EMI–pressed copies also exist with die–cut, four–prong centres. Sleeves as supplied with EMI–era pressings still include the by then incorrect Ivor Court address. Number 6 in the UK EP charts.

IMEP 002 THE McCOYS: Hits Vol. 1: The McCoys

1. Hang On Sloopy
2. Up And Down

1. You Make Me Feel (So Good)
2. Runaway

Rel: Dec 1966[1]
RRP: 11/6[1]

Picture sleeve. Two hits, yes, but not both in the UK.

IMEP 003 THE McCOYS: Hits Vol. 2: The McCoys

1. Don't Worry Mother, Your Son's Heart Is Pure
2. Fever

1. Come On Let's Go
2. Sorrow

Rel: Dec 1966[1]
RRP: 11/6[1]

Picture sleeve. The rear of the sleeve and both labels include the Bang Records logo. Two hits, yes, but ditto.

IMEP 004 CHRIS FARLOWE: Hits

1. Out Of Time
2. Headlines

1. Ride On Baby
2. Think

Rel: Dec 1966[1]
RRP: 11/6[1]

Picture sleeve.

IMLP/IMSP/IMCP sequence LPs

The IMLP sequence comprised mono LPs and was amended to IMSP for stereo releases, with many records being issued in both formats. The curiosity nowadays is the IMCP variation. The "C" stands for "Compatible" – this means that the LP was pressed to play stereo on stereo players and true mono on mono players. The format didn't last very long.

IMLP 001 THE McCOYS: Hang On Sloopy

1. Meet The McCoys
2. Hang On Sloopy
3. Fever
4. Sorrow
5. If You Tell A Lie
6. I Don't Mind
7. Stubborn Kind Of Fellow

1. I Can't Help Falling In Love
2. All I Really Want To Do
3. Papa's Got A Brand New Bag
4. I Can't Explain It
5. High Heel Sneakers
6. Stormy Monday Blues

Rel: Dec 1965[13]/ Sep 1966[14]

The sleeve and labels include the Bang Records logo. Track listing above as per sleeve. The September release date for all LPs up to IMLP 005 as documented in EMI's January 1970 *Export Numerical Catalogue Service* listings seems to be an arbitrary–assigned (incorrect) blanket release date for almost all Philips–era releases inherited by EMI.

IMLP 002 SAM COOKE: The Wonderful World Of Sam Cooke

1. That's Heaven to Me
2. Deep River
3. I Thank God
4. Heaven Is My Home
5. God Is Standing By
6. Pass Me Not

1. Steal Away
2. Must Jesus Bear His Cross Alone
3. Lead Me Jesus
4. Trouble In Mind
5. Sometimes
6. Somebody

Rel: Feb 1966[13]/ Sep 1966[14]

Flipback sleeve. Sleeves exist with "Stereo" printed in a box on the front but with mono catalogue number and mono record. Not the same as the LP released under this title on the US Keen label.

IMLP/IMSP 003 ARANBEE POP SYMPHONY ORCHESTRA: Today's Pop Symphony (MONO/STEREO)

1. There's A Place
2. Rag Doll
3. I Got You, Babe
4. We Can Work It Out
5. Play With Fire

1. Mother's Little Helper
2. In The Midnight Hour
3. Take It Or Leave It
4. Sittin' On A Fence
5. I Don't Want To Go On Without You

Rel: Feb 1966[13]/ Sep 1966[14]

Flipback sleeve. Mono version credits Philips on labels but stereo version does not.

IMLP/IMSP 004 MARK MURPHY: Who Can I Turn To? (MONO/STEREO)

1. Who Can I Turn To? (When Nobody Needs Me) (From "Roar Of The Greasepaint – Smell Of The Crowd")
2. I Wanna Be Around
3. That's What Makes A Girl
4. Cotton Fields
5. A Wonderful Day Like Today (From "Roar Of The Greasepaint – Smell Of The Crowd")
6. You'd Better Love Me (From "High Spirits")

1. There Is A Time (Le Temps)
2. My Kind Of Girl
3. This Train
4. Star Sounds
5. In Love For The Very First Time
6. Talk To Me Baby (From "Foxy")

Rel: Feb 1966[13]/ Sep 1966[14]

Flipback sleeve. Subtitled *& 11 other great standards* on the sleeve. Stereo version sleeve includes mention of availability of a book, titled *The Immediate Records Success Story*, which was free to anyone sending a stamped addressed envelope (also advertised on the sleeves for IMLP 002, IMLP/SP 003 and IMLP 005). Oddly, the mono version sleeve calls the book "The Immediate Art Records Success Story." Mono version credits Philips on labels but stereo version does not.

IMLP 005 CHRIS FARLOWE: 14 Things To Think About

1. Think
2. My Colouring Book
3. Lipstick Traces
4. Summertime
5. That's No Big Thing
6. Don't Play That Song
7. Looking For You

1. It's All Over Now, Baby Blue
2. I Just Don't Know What To Do With Myself
3. Rockin' Pneumonia
4. Why Don't You Change Your Ways
5. My Girl Josephine
6. Yesterday
7. Don't Just Look At Me

Rel: Mar 1966[13]/ Sep 1966[14]

Number 19 in the UK charts. An export–only compilation of selected tracks from this album along with both sides of IM 016 appeared on EMI's Regal export label as *Chris Farlowe* (REG 2025), probably in 1968. Not, strictly speaking a UK release, so not otherwise documented.

IMLP/IMSP 006 CHRIS FARLOWE: The Art Of Chris Farlowe (MONO/STEREO)

1. What Became Of The Broken Hearted
2. We're Doing Fine
3. Life Is But Nothing
4. Paint It Black
5. Cuttin' In
6. Open The Door To Your Heart
7. Out Of Time

1. North South East West
2. You're So Good For Me
3. It Was Easier To Hurt Her
4. I'm Free
5. I've Been Loving You Too Long
6. Reach Out I'll Be There
7. Ride On Baby

Rel: Dec 1966[1]/ Nov 1966[14]
RRP:33/6[1]

The sleeve advertises both Farlowe's first LP and the two EPs. The sleeve does not include the catalogue number prefix, but just includes "006": this is presumably to preclude having to print separate sleeves for mono and stereo versions – cheapskates! Number 37 in the UK charts.

IMLP/IMSP 007 TWICE AS MUCH: Own Up (MONO/STEREO)

1. I Have A Love
2. Help
3. Is This What I Get For Loving You Baby?
4. Night Time Girl
5. Life Is But Nothing
6. The Spinning Wheel
7. Happy Times

1. Sha La La La Lee
2. We Can Work It Out
3. As Tears Go By
4. The Time Is Right
5. The Summer's Ending
6. Play With Fire
7. Why Can't They All Go And Leave Me Alone?

Rel: Dec 1966[1]/ Nov 1966[14]
RRP:33/6[1]

The sleeve does not seem to include the catalogue number (the spine is the only bit I haven't viewed): this is presumably to preclude having to print separate sleeves for mono and stereo versions.

IMLP/IMSP 008 SMALL FACES: The Small Faces (MONO/STEREO)

1. (Tell Me) Have You Ever Seen Me
2. Something I Want To Tell You
3. Feeling Lonely
4. Happy Boys Happy
5. Things Are Going To Get Better
6. My Way Of Giving
7. Green Circles

1. Become Like You
2. Get Yourself Together
3. All Our Yesterdays
4. Talk To You
5. Show Me The Way
6. Up The Wooden Hills To Bedfordshire
7. Eddie's Dreaming

Rel: Jun 1967[14]

Flipback sleeve. Number 12 in the UK charts.

IMCP 009 BILLY NICHOLLS: Would You Believe?

Side 1	Side 2	
1. Would You Believe?	1. London Social Degree	**Rel:** Apr 1968[14]
2. Come Again	2. Portobello Road	
3. Life Is Short	3. Question Mark	
4. Feeling Easy	4. Being Happy	
5. Daytime Girl	5. Girl From New York	
6. Daytime Girl (Coda)	6. It Brings Me Down	

Mono/stereo compatible release. Generally thought to have been withdrawn or never pressed, apart from for promotional purposes, until one or two copies started to creep out of the woodwork. Sorry to blow a good theory out of the water, but the LP was still listed as available from EMI in (probably) early 1970[14]. There's probably a warehouse full of boxes of the LP somewhere! The last copy spotted for sale sold for around £8,000, which was a good few thousand up on the previous sale.

IMCP 010 CHRIS FARLOWE: The Best Of Chris Farlowe Vol. 1

Side 1	Side 2	
1. Paint It Black	1. The Last Goodbye	**Rel:** May 1968[14]/
2. Paperman Fly In The Sky	2. Ride On Baby	Jun 1968[1]
3. Yesterday's Papers	3. Headlines	**RRP:** 37/8[1]
4. Everyone Makes A Mistake	4. What Have I Been Doing	
5. Moanin'	5. My Way Of Giving	
6. Out Of Time	6. Handbags And Gladrags	

Mono/stereo compatible release.

IMLP/IMSP 011 P. P. ARNOLD: The First Lady of Immediate (MONO/STEREO)

Side 1	Side 2	
1. (If You Think You're) Groovy	1. Everything Is Gonna Be Alright	**Rel:** Apr 1968[14]
2. Something Beautiful Happened	2. Treat Me Like A Lady	
3. Born To Be Together	3. Would You Believe	
4. Am I Still Dreaming	4. Life Is But Nothing	
5. Though It Hurts Me Badly	5. Speak To Me	
6. First Cut Is The Deepest	6. The Time Has Come	

Rumours abound that this was never released; other rumours state only a limited release. Not so in either case – this record was listed as available at least until January 1970 in both mono and stereo versions[14].

IMLP/IMSP 012 SMALL FACES: Ogden's Nut Gone Flake (MONO/STEREO)

Side 1	Side 2	
1. Ogdens' Nut Gone Flake	1. Happiness Stan	**Rel:** May 1968[14]
2. Afterglow	2. Rollin' Over	
3. Long Agos And Worlds Apart	3. The Hungry Intruder	
4. Rene	4. The Journey	
5. Song Of A Baker	5. Mad John	
6. Lazy Sunday	6. Happydaystoytown	

Circular, fold–out sleeve. Side 1 label is credited as "Ogden's Nut Gone Flake" whilst side 2 is credited as "Happiness Stan". Mono and stereo copies appeared on both lilac and pink label designs. Lilac labels include the text, "FOR AMAZING RESULTS THIS RECORD SHOULD BE PLAYED AT FULL VOLUME" around the top rim of the label, but this does not appear on pink label copies, even though early pink labels otherwise have the same text layout and design. Also listed as "Small Faces New Album" with "If You Think You're Groovy" (no brackets) listed in place of *Rene*[14]. Perhaps that denotes the originally–planned track listing, which then failed to be corrected in subsequent EMI listings.

Lilac and early pink label copies have drastically different text layout and design to that of later pink label copies. The "Sold in the U.K." text is conspicuous by its absence on all labels viewed. Later stereo copies have light pink labels instead of the more normal dark pink. *Afterglow* misses out the "(Of Your Love)" but includes acoustic intro (however, it cuts directly from the drum fill to the next track, thus making it different to every other release). UK number 1.

IMCP 013 TWICE AS MUCH: That's All

Side 1	Side 2	
1. Sittin' On A Fence	1. True Story	**Rel:** Apr 1968[14]/ May 1968[13]
2. Hey Girl	2. Simplified	
3. Listen	3. Step Out Of Line	
4. You're So Good For Me	4. You'll Never Get To Heaven	
5. Green Circles	5. Crystal Ball	
6. Life Is But Nothing/Happy Times/ Do You Wanna Dance	6. The Coldest Night Of The Year	

Compatible release, though, oddly, copies exist with IMSP 013 on labels but IMCP 013 on sleeve; matrix numbers on the stereo copy are IMSP 013–1Y and 2Y as opposed to the more usual IMCP 013–1C and 2C. On the stereo version, the medley is replaced by *Baby I Want You.* Also, the stereo version has side 2 credits as above on sleeve but playing order 2, 5, 1, 4, 6, 3 (as per label). Curious, especially as only the compatible release is listed in later EMI trade listings[14]. Best guess is that the stereo version was briefly released before the track listing order error was spotted and that the opportunity was also taken to replace the final side 1 track and make it a compatible release instead of just stereo. As I said, this is just a guess!

IMLP 014 VARIOUS ARTISTS: Blues Anytime Vol. 1

Side 1	Side 2	
1. I'm Your Witchdoctor (John Mayall And The Bluesbreakers)	1. Telephone Blues (John Mayall And The Bluesbreakers)	**Rel:** Apr 1968[1/14] **RRP:** 37/8[1]
2. Snake Drive (Eric Clapton)	2. You Don't Love Me (T.S. Mc Phee)	
3. Ain't Gonna Cry No More (T.S. McPhee)	3. West Coast Idea (Eric Clapton)	
	4. Ain't Seen No Whisky (Jo–Ann Kelly)	
4. I Tried (Savoy Brown Blues Band)	5. Flapjacks (Stone's Masonry)	
5. Tribute to Elmore (Eric Clapton)	6. Cold Blooded Woman (Savoy Brown Blues Band)	
6. I Feel So Good (Jo–Ann Kelly)		

Subtitled *An Anthology of British Blues.* Flipback sleeve (there is also a non–flipback version on the later pink label design). Sleeve states, "Album produced in conjunction with BLUE HORIZON RECORDS". Side 1 later issued as side 1 of IMAL 03/04 and side 2 later issued as side 1 of IMAL 05/06. The Savoy Brown and Stone's Masonry tracks, and at least one T.S. McPhee track, were originally issued by Purdah: track 3, side 1 issued as *Ain't Gonna Cry No Mo'* as b–side of *Someone to Love Me* (45–3501); *I Tried* issued as a–side (45–3503), credited to "Savoy Brown's Blues Band"; *Flapjacks* released as a–side (45–3504).

IMCP 015 VARIOUS ARTISTS: Blues Anytime Vol. 2

Side 1	Side 2	
1. On Top Of The World (John Mayall And The Bluesbreakers)	1. Freight Loader (Eric Clapton And Jimmy Page)	**Rel:** May 1968[14]/ Jun 1968[1] **RRP:** 37/8[1]
2. Someone To Love Me (T.S. McPhee)	2. Look Down At My Woman (Jeremy Spencer)	
3. I Can't Quit You Baby (Savoy Brown Blues Band)	3. Roll 'Em Pete (Dharma Blues Band)	
4. Draggin' My Tail (Eric Clapton With Jimmy Page)	4. Choker (Eric Clapton And Jimmy Page)	
5. Dealing With The Devil (Dharma Blues Band)	5. True Blue (Savoy Brown Blues Band)	
6. Who's Knocking At Your Door (Jeremy Spencer)	6. When You Got A Good Friend (T. S. McPhee)	

Mono/stereo compatible release. Track details above sourced from the original US release – memory tells me that the label and rear sleeve text is the same as on the UK release. Track 1, side 1 is credited to "John Mayall And The Bluesbreakers" on the label and "John Mayall And The Bluesbreakers With Eric Clapton" on the sleeve. Sleeve states "Album produced in conjunction with BLUE HORIZON RECORDS". Side 1 later issued as side 3 of IMAL 05/06 and side 2 later issued as side 4 of IMAL 03/04. *Who's Knocking* is really by Spencer's old band, The Levi Set, recorded at Decca in Spring 1967. Track 3, side 1, is evidently credited as "Can't Quit You Baby" without the "I" – not confirmed.

IMLP/IMSP 016 THE NICE: The Thoughts Of Emerlist Davjack (MONO/STEREO)

1. Flower King Of Flies	1. War And Peace	**Rel:** May 1968[14]
2. The Thoughts Of Emerlist Davjack	2. Tantalising Maggie	
3. Bonnie K	3. Dawn	
4. Rondo	4. The Cry Of Eugene	

Mono and stereo copies exist on the lilac label, but it is unclear whether mono copies exist on the pink label (probably yes). Pink label copies exist with and without "SOLD IN U.K." text, those without having light pink labels instead of the more normal dark pink. These late 1969 copies include the original New Oxford Street address credit instead of the new Gloucester Place one – either an oversight or the existence of a glut of original sleeves. Sleeve misses out "The" on track 2, side 1.

Alternative versions of most tracks, along with alternative versions of several other Immediate–era tracks, were issued by Charisma in 1972 as *Autumn '67 to Spring '68* (CS 1) and subsequently reissued by Hallmark as *The Nice Featuring America*, probably in 1978 (SHM 917). These are not listed amongst the reissues because these versions were never issued by Immediate in the first place.

The LP below was the first issued on the pink label design as were all all subsequent LPs, except for IMSP 018, which was issued out of sequence on the lilac label design.

IMSP 017 P. P. ARNOLD: Kafunta

1. Letter To Bill	1. It'll Never Happen Again	**Rel:** Aug 1968[14]/ Oct 1968[1]
Kafunta One	*Kafunta Two*	**RRP:** 37/8[1]
2. God Only Knows	2. As Tears Go By	
3. Eleanor Rigby	*Kafunta Three*	
4. Yesterday	3. To Love Somebody	
5. Angel Of The Morning	4. Dreamin'	
	Kafunta Four	
	5. Welcome Home	

Labels list the *Kafunta* sections in a different type face to the main tracks, but these are not listed on the sleeve. On labels, *Kafunta One* and *Kafunta Four* both have writer credits "(Mark, Hopkins)" but *Kafunta Two* and *Kafunta Three* have the more enigmatic "(Nice)" and "(Lovely)" respectively.

IMSP 018 DUNCAN BROWNE: Give Me Take You

1. Give Me Take You	1. On The Bombsite	**Rel:** Jul 1968[11/14]
2. Ninepence Worth Of Walking	2. I Was You Weren't	
3. Dwarf In A Tree (A Cautionary Tale)	3. Gabilan	
4. The Ghost Walks	4. Alfred Bell	
5. Waking You (Part One)	5. The Death Of Neil	
6. Chloe In The Garden		
7. Waking You (Part Two)		

Lyric sheet. This was the last LP issued on the lilac label design.

IMLP 019 VARIOUS ARTISTS: Blues Anytime Vol. 3

1. Someday Baby (Cyril Davies And The All Stars)	1. Miles Road (Eric Clapton And Jimmy Page)	**Rel:** Nov 1968[14]
2. Steelin' (The All Stars Featuring Jeff Beck)	2. Porcupine Juice (Santa Barbara Machine Head)	
3. L.A. Breakdown (The All Stars Featuring Jimmy Page)	3. Albert (Santa Barbara Machine Head)	
4. Chuckles (The All Stars Featuring Jeff Beck)	4. Rubber Monkey (Santa Barbara Machine Head)	
5. Down In The Boots (The All Stars Featuring Jimmy Page)	5. Howlin' For My Darling (Stuff Smith)	
6. Piano Shuffle (The All Stars Featuring Nicky Hopkins)		

Track and artist details from labels. Sleeve credits album as "Vol. 3", whilst labels credit it as "Vol. III". Side 1 later issued as side 3 of IMAL 03/04 and side 2 later issued as side 4 of IMAL 05/06.

IMSP 020 *THE NICE: Ars Longa Vita Brevis*

Side 1	Side 2	
1. Daddy Where Did I Come From	1. Symphony For Group And Orchestra	**Rel:** Nov 1968[14]
2. Little Arabella	a. Prelude	
3. Happy Freuds	b. 1st Movement: Awakening	
4. Intermezzo From The Karelia Suite	c. 2nd Movement: Realization	
5. Don Edito El Gruva	d. 3rd Movement: Acceptance "Brandenburger"	
	e. 4th Movement: Denial	
	f. Coda – Extension To The Big Note	

Flipback and non–flipback sleeves. All flipback sleeves viewed include the New Oxford Street address, whilst all non–flipback sleeves viewed include the Gloucester Place address. Two label variations: one with "SOLD IN U.K." text as one long line, centre, beneath the Immediate logo; one with the text spread over three lines to the left of the label. Late, non–flipback copies exist without text. Label includes overall track title for side 2 as above, whilst sleeve credits "Ars Longa Vita Brevis". Sleeve doesn't include the colons in the side 2 part titles. Trivia: track 5, side 1 appeared on a Gong fan club tape (*Over The Top*) along with a snippet from the second LP by (Arthur Brown's) Kingdom Come.

IMLP 021 *CHRIS FARLOWE: The Last Goodbye*

Side 1	Side 2	
1. The Last Goodbye	1. Dawn	**Rel:** May 1969[14]
2. Think	2. Looking For You	
3. In The Midnight Hour	3. It Was Easier To Hurt Her	
4. Mr. Pitful	4. Don't Just Look At Me	
5. Satisfaction	5. April Was The Month	
6. Who Can I Turn To	6. Handbags And Gladrags	
7. You're So Good For Me	7. Life Is But Nothing	

Label credits "Satisfaction" whilst the sleeve credits "(I Can't Get No) Satisfaction".

IMLP 022 *SMALL FACES: In Memoriam (EXPORT–ONLY?)*

Side 1	Side 2	
1. Small Faces Live	1. Collibosher	**Rel:** May 1969[13]
2. Rollin' Over	2. Call It Something Nice	
3. If I Were A Carpenter	3. Red Balloon	
4. Every Little Bit Hurts	4. Wide Eyed Girl On The Wall	
5. All Or Nothing	5. The Autumn Stone	
6. Tin Soldier		

Long thought to have been a European–only release with UK copies pressed for export only. However, in the 1990s a fully–fledged UK pressing was reported in *Record Collector*. UK–pressed export copies on the pink label with "Sold in U.K." text, housed in sleeve with UK EMI credits and German catalogue number (1 C 048–90 201). Side 1 live, with the first track being 19 or so seconds of introduction. Not listed as available in the UK in the January 1970 *EMI Records Export Numerical Catalogue Service* list, which would suggest that this was never intended for UK release even if one or two apparently full UK copies seem to exist.

IMSP 023 *AMEN CORNER: The National West Coast Live Explosion Company*

Side 1	Side 2	
1. Introduction: Macarthur Park	1. Penny Lane	**Rel:** Aug 1969[14]/
2. Baby Do The Philly Dog	2. High In The Sky	Dec 1969[1]/
3. You're My Girl (I Don't Want To Discuss It)	3. Gin House	5 Sep 1969
4. Shake A Tail Feather	4. Bend Me, Shape Me	**RRP:** 37/6[1]
5. So Fine	5. (If Paradise Is) Half As Nice	
6. (Our Love) Is In The Pocket		

Cassette/reel–to–reel/8–track: TC–IMSP 023/TD–IMSP 023/8X-IMSP 023 **Rel:** Dec 1969[14]
Labels do not include, "Sold in U.K." text. Number 19 in the UK charts. December LP release date as advised belatedly (possibly when tape versions were advised); September release date as listed on the AS 3 promotional sampler. New, unplayed copies of this LP regularly cropped up for sale up until the late 1970s (I bought my first copy in the *Threshold* shop in Swindon in 1978, if memory serves).

IMLP 024 *VARIOUS ARTISTS: Blues Leftovers*

1. The Next Milestone (Albert Lee Vocals T. Colton)
2. Somebody's Going To Get Their Head Kicked In Tonight (Earl Vince And The Valiants)
3. New Death Matter (Dave Kelly)
4. Back Water Blues (Jo–Ann Kelly)
5. So Much To Say (Rod Stewart)
6. Married Woman Blues (Dave Kelly)

1. Water On My Fire (Albert Lee Vocals Paul Williams)
2. Keep Your Hands Out Of My Pockets (Jo–Ann Kelly)
3. Alabama Woman (Dave Kelly)
4. Crosstown Link (Albert Lee)
5. All Night Long (Dave Kelly)
6. Down And Dirty (Simon And Steve)

Rel: Oct 1969[14]/ Dec 1969[1]
RRP: 37/6[1]

Chris Farlowe namechecked on sleeve by mistake. No artist credits on labels. Side 1 later issued as side 2 of IMAL 03/04 and side 2 later issued as side 2 of IMAL 05/06. Despite title, this was volume 4 of the *Blues Anytime* series, as stated on the rear sleeve (labels credit the album as "Blues Leftovers Vol. 4"). Sleeve also states "A Conman Production"! December LP release date as advised belatedly.

IMSP 025 *HUMBLE PIE: As Safe As Yesterday Is*

1. Desperation
2. Stick Shift
3. Buttermilk Boy
4. Growing Closer
5. As Safe As Yesterday Is

1. Bang?
2. Alabama '69
3. I'll Go Alone
4. A Nifty Little Number Like You
5. What You Will

Rel: Aug 1969[14]/ Dec 1969[1]
RRP: 37/6[1]

Cassette/reel–to–reel/8–track: TC–IMSP 025/TD–IMSP 025/8X-IMSP 025 **Rel:** Dec 1969[14]
Inner sleeve. *Growing Closer* has the sub–credit, *(Mac's song)* on the inner sleeve, commemorating the fact that the song was written by Ian McLagan. December LP release date as advised belatedly.

IMSP 026 *THE NICE: Nice*

1. Azrael Revisited
2. Hang On To A Dream
3. Diary Of An Empty Day
4. For Example

1. Rondo ('69)
2. She Belongs To Me

Rel: Aug 1969[14]/ Dec 1969[1]/ 5 Sep 1969
RRP: 37/6[1]

Cassette/reel–to–reel/8–track: TC–IMSP 026/TD–IMSP 026/8X-IMSP 026 **Rel:** Dec 1969[14]
Two sleeve variations with different gatefold construction (different printers perhaps): early copies have Immediate logo and address, plus stereo blurb along the bottom, left of the inner gatefold; later copies have these printed at 90° down the inner spine. Labels do not include "Sold in U.K." text. Sleeve and side 2 label include the credit, "Recorded live at Fillmore East, New York" (no comma on sleeve credit). Sleeve credits track 1, side 2 as "Rondo '69'" (i.e. no brackets). Also exists with very light pink label as well as more usual dark pink. December LP release date as advised belatedly; September release date as listed on the AS 4 promotional LP sampler single. Number 3 in UK charts.

IMSP 027 *HUMBLE PIE: Town And Country*

1. Take Me Back
2. The Sad Bag Of Shaky Jake
3. The Light Of Love
4. Cold Lady
5. Down Home Again
6. Ollie Ollie

1. Every Mothers Son
2. Heartbeat
3. Only You Can Say
4. Silver Tongue
5. Home And Away

Rel: Oct 1969[14]/ Dec 1969[1]
RRP: 37/6[1]

Cassette/reel–to–reel/8–track: TC–IMSP 027/TD–IMSP 027/8X-IMSP 027 **Rel:** Dec 1969[14]
Inner sleeve. Track 3, side 2 credited as "Only You Can See" on inner sleeve. Track 1, side 2 has an apostrophe on one side of the inner sleeve but not the other. Label does not include the apostrophe. December LP release date as advised belatedly.

IMSP 028 ***AMEN CORNER: Farewell To The Real Magnificent Seven***

Side 1	Side 2	
1. Lady Riga	1. The Weight	**Rel:** Oct 1969[14]/ Dec 1969[1]
2. Hello Susie	2. (If Paradise Is) Half As Nice	
3. Proud Mary	3. Welcome To The Club	**RRP:** 37/6[1]
4. At Last I've Found Someone To Love	4. Recess	
5. Scream And Scream Again	5. When We Make Love	
6. Sanitation	6. Things Ain't What They Used To Be	
7. Mr. Nonchalant	7. Get Back	

Cassette/reel–to–reel/8–track: TC–IMSP 028/TD–IMSP 028/8X-IMSP 028 **Rel:** Dec 1969[14]
December LP release date as advised belatedly.

IMLYIN sequence LPs

IMLYIN 1 ***VARIOUS ARTISTS: Immediate Lets You In***

Side 1	Side 2	
1. Afterglow (Small Faces)	1. Rondo (The Nice)	**Rel:** Jan 1969[14]/ Mar 1969[1]
2. Handbags And Gladrags (Chris Farlowe)	2. Someday Baby (Cyril Davies And The All Stars)	**RRP:** 19/11[1]
3. Happy Freuds (The Nice)	3. God Only Knows (P.P. Arnold)	
4. Telephone Blues (John Mayall And The Bluesbreakers)	4. The Death Of Neil (Duncan Browne)	
5. Draggin' My Tail (Eric Clapton With Jimmy Page)		

There are two label variations: one has the "Sold in U.K." text as one long line, centre, underneath the Immediate logo; the other has the text spread over three lines to the left of the label. The catalogue number is "IMLYIN" on the sleeve spine but "IMLYIN 1" on the labels. (Is there a bit of a coded message to this series of letters, other than being made up from letters from the album title, that is? Try putting a space after the "M".) This is the only place to find the acoustic intro to "Afterglow". This version then fades out on the drum fill and so is different to both the single version and to that included on "Ogden's Nut Gone Flake". Also, the track is credited as "Afterglow" only, without the "(Of Your Love)" sub–title.

IMLYIN 2 ***VARIOUS ARTISTS: Happy To Be Part Of The Industry Of Human Happiness***

Side 1	Side 2	
1. So Fine (Amen Corner)	1. Cold Lady (Humble Pie)	**Rel:** Oct 1969[14]/ Dec 1969[1]
2. Man Of The World (Fleetwood Mac)	2. Hang On To A Dream (The Nice)	
3. Water On My Fire (Albert Lee)	3. On Top Of The World (John Mayall's Bluesbreakers And Eric Clapton)	**RRP:** 15/–[1]
4. Tribute To Elmore (Eric Clapton And Jimmy Page)	4. Recess (Amen Corner)	
5. Alabama '69 (Humble Pie)	5. Lazy Sunday (Small Faces)	

Labels do not include "Sold in U.K." text. Labels credit on which LPs each track can be found. *Cold Lady* is credited as coming from the LP, "Humble Pie", instead of *Town and Country*.

IMAL sequence double LPs

IMAL 01/02 *SMALL FACES: The Autumn Stone*

Record 1: side 1
1. Here Comes The Nice
2. The Autumn Stone
3. Collibosher
4. All Or Nothing*
5. Red Balloon
6. Lazy Sunday

Record 1: side 2
1. Call It Something Nice
2. I Can't Make It
3. Afterglow Of Your Love
4. Sha La La La Lee
5. The Universal

Rel: Sep 1969[14]/ Dec 1969[1]
RRP: 39/6[1]

Record 2: side 1
1. Rollin' Over*
2. If I Were A Carpenter*
3. Every Little Bit Hurts*
4. My Mind's Eye
5. Tin Soldier
6. Just Passing

Record 2: side 2
1. Itchycoo Park
2. Hey Girl
3. Wide Eyed Girl On The Wall
4. Whacha Gonna Do About It
5. Wham Bam Thank You Man

Track 1, side 1 credited as "Comes" on label and "Come" on sleeve (the latter is correct). *Afterglow of Your Love* (without brackets) has acoustic intro and fade out on drum fill. Album sequence seems to have been altered at some point – LP 1, side 2 has "IMA L02 1Y–2G" crossed out and "IMAL. 01 2Y–2G" added below, which matches the original German issue where the UK sides 2 and 3 are reversed. Tracks with asterisk are (slowed down) live recordings from Newcastle City Hall. Dutch copies exist in what look suspiciously like UK–manufactured sleeves (with UK catalogue numbers).

IMAL 03/04 *VARIOUS ARTISTS: An Anthology Of British Blues Vol. 1*

Record 1: side 1
1. I'm Your Witchdoctor (John Mayall And The Bluesbreakers Featuring Eric Clapton)
2. Snake Drive (Eric Clapton And Jimmy Page)
3. Ain't Gonna Cry No More (Tony S. McPhee)
4. I Tried (Savoy Brown Blues Band)
5. Tribute To Elmore (Eric Clapton And Jimmy Page)
6. I Feel So Good (Jo–Ann Kelly)

Record 1: side 2
1. The Next Milestone (Albert Lee Vocals – T. Colton)
2. Somebody's Gonna Get Their Head Kicked In Tonite (Earl Vince And The Valiants)
3. New Death Matter (Dave Kelly)
4. Backwater Blues (Jo–Ann Kelly)
5. So Much To Say (Rod Stewart)
6. Married Woman Blues (Dave Kelly)

Rel: Nov 1969[14]/ Dec 1969[1]
RRP: 39/6[1]

Record 2: side 1
1. Someday Baby (Cyril Davies And The All–Stars)
2. Steelin' (The All Stars Featuring Jeff Beck)
3. L. A. Breakdown (The All Stars Featuring Jimmy Page)
4. Chuckles (The All Stars Featuring Jeff Beck)
5. Down In The Boots (The All Stars Featuring Jimmy Page)
5. Piano Shuffle (The All Stars Featuring Nicky Hopkins)

Record 2: side 2
1. Freight Loader (Eric Clapton And Jimmy Page)
2. Look Down At My Woman (Jeremy Spencer)
3. Roll 'Em Pete (Dharma Blues Band)
4. Choker (Eric Clapton And Jimmy Page)
5. True Story (Savoy Brown Blues Band)
6. When You Got A Good Friend (Tony S. McPhee)

No "Sold in U.K." text or artist credits on labels. Side 1 originally issued as side 1 of IMLP 014; side 2 originally issued as side 1 of IMLP 024; side 3 originally issued as side 1 of IMLP 019; side 4 originally issued as side 2 of IMCP 015.

IMAL 05/06 ***VARIOUS ARTISTS: An Anthology Of British Blues Vol. 2***

Rel: Nov 1969[14]/ Dec 1969[1]
RRP: 39/6[1]

Record 1: side 1

Telephone Blues (John Mayall And The Bluesbreakers)
2. You Don't Love Me (T.S. McPhee)
3. West Coast Idea (Eric Clapton)
4. Ain't Seen No Whisky (Jo–Ann Kelly)
5. Flapjacks (Stone's Masonry)
6. Cold Blooded Woman (Savoy Brown Blues Band)

Record 1: side 2

1. Water On My Fire (Albert Lee Vocals Paul Williams)
2. Keep Your Hands Out Of My Pockets (Jo–Ann Kelly)
3. Alabama Woman (Dave Kelly)
4. Crosstown Link (Albert Lee)
5. All Night Long (Dave Kelly)
6. Down And Dirty (Simon And Steve)

Record 2: side 1

1. On Top Of The World (John Mayalls Bluesbreakers)
2. Someone to Love Me (T.S. McPhee)
3. Can't Quit You Baby (Savoy Brown Blues Band)
4. Draggin' My Tail (Eric Clapton With Jimmy Page)
5. Dealing With The Devil (Dharma Blues Band)
6. Who's Knocking (Jeremy Spencer)

Record 2: side 2

1. Miles Road (Eric Clapton And Jimmy Page)
2. Porcupine Juice (Santa Barbara Machine Head)
3. Albert (Santa Barbara Machine Head)
4. Rubber Monkey (Santa Barbara Machine Head)
5. Howlin' (Stuff Smith)

No "Sold in U.K." text or artist credits on labels. Side 1 originally issued as side 2 of IMLP 014; side 2 originally issued as side 2 of IMLP 024; side 3 originally issued as side 1 of IMCP 015; side 4 originally issued as side 2 of IMLP 019. Originally-planned sequencing of sides may have been different – the side 1 matrix is "IMAL 03 2Y–1G" with "03 2Y" scratched out and replaced with "05 1Y". Similarly, the side 3 matrix is "IMAL 04 1Y–1G" with "04" scratched out and replaced with "06".

AS sequence 7" promotional LP samplers

AS 1 ***SMALL FACES: Excerpts From Small Faces L.P. IMLP/SP. 008***

Dist: 1967

One–sided, EMI–pressed, promotional sampler for the "Small Faces" LP, IMLP/IMSP 008. "ALBUM SAMPLER" appears above "SMALL FACES", both in the same point size. Under this in smaller point size is "Excerpts From Small Faces L.P. IMLP/SP. 008". "DEMONSTRATION SAMPLE NOT FOR SALE" appears directly below the "Immediate" logo. Upside–down, above the "AS. 1" catalogue number, and in smaller point size, is a "SFP 1" matrix number. The record includes spoken links – oddly the spoken monologue only advertises the mono version of the album. Excerpts are from "Get Yourself Together", "Green Circles", "Talk To You", "All Our Yesterdays" and "Up The Wooden Hills To Bedfordshire".

AS 2 ***THE NICE: Excerpts From The Nice L.P. IMLP/SP 016***

Dist: 1968

"ALBUM SAMPLER" appears above "THE THOUGHTS OF EMERLIST DAVJACK", both in the same point size. Underneath in smaller point size is "Excerpts From The Nice L.P. IMLP/SP 016". "DEMONSTRATION SAMPLE NOT FOR SALE" appears directly below the "Immediate" logo. Upside–down, above the "AS 2" catalogue number, and in smaller point size, is the "SF P2" matrix number. Copies exist with EMI factory sample stickers on the a–side label. Includes spoken links by John Peel ("…the Nice came together in a void, and will be here when the rest are in pantomime in Wolverhampton..."). Excerpts from *Bonnie 'K'*, *Rondo*, *The Cry of Eugene*, *War and Peace*, *Flower King of Flies*, and *Tantalising Maggie*.

AS 3 ***AMEN CORNER: So Fine/So Fine***

Dist: 1969

Label includes the text, "(From the album 'The National West Coast Live Explosion Company' IMSP 023)". "SINGLE SAMPLER ONLY" appears above the track credit. The label is the white demo design with large red "A", but without "DEMONSTRATION SAMPLE" text. Upside–down, above the "AS 3" catalogue number, and in smaller point size, is a "SF P3" matrix number. Includes release date of "5.9.69" for the LP. Four–proing and solid–centred copies exist.

AS 4 ***THE NICE: She Belongs To Me/She Belongs To Me***

Dist: 1969

Label includes the text, "(From the album 'Nice' IMSP 026)". Labels include the text "SINGLE SAMPLER ONLY". Copies exist with EMI factory sample stickers on the a–side label. Upside–down, above the "AS 4" catalogue number, and in smaller point size, is a "SF P4" matrix number. Includes release date of "5.9.69" for the LP.

Trade–only 12" double–sided acetate

No cat. no. ***SPOKEN WORD: Meditation Con***

Distributed: Christmas 1968

Documented in Simon Spence's *Immediate* book, this evidently comprised a short–run of 200 copies, which were sent to managing directors of all UK record and publishing companies. Subtitled "comment on the state of the industry", it comprised secretly–taped interviews with Mike Sloman, UK head of MCA, and was intended to make a fool of him. Not a nice thing to do.

INSTANT

INLP/INSP sequence LPs

INLP 001 ***OST: European Cup The Date...May 29th 1968 The Match... Manchester United V Benfica***

Side 1	Side 2	
1. Highlights First Half	1. Extra Time	**Rel:** Aug 1968[14]
2. Highlights Second Half		

Die–cut, circular sleeve, designed to look like a football. Evidently also came in outer, plastic packaging. Title above as printed on front sleeve. Also listed as *Recorded Highlights: European Cup Final 1968*. Released by arrangement with BBC Radio Enterprises. Commentators are Alan Clarke and Peter Jones, with a summary by John Campion.

INLP 002 ***VARIOUS ARTISTS/OST: Tonite Let's All Make Love In London***

Side 1	Side 2	
1. Intersteller Overdrive (Pink Floyd)	1. Intersteller Overdrive (Pink Floyd)	**Rel:** Nov 1968[14]
2. Changing Of The Guards (The Marquess Of Kensington)	2. Winter Is Blue (Vashti)	
3. Night Time Girl (Twice As Much)	3. Paint It Black (Chris Farlowe)	
4. Out Of Time (Chris Farlowe)	4. Here Come The Nice (Small Faces)	
	5. Intersteller Overdrive (Pink Floyd)	

The famous 'swinging' London film soundtrack LP from the Peter Whitehead film. Songs interspersed with spoken word from: Allen Ginsberg (a poem); Alan Aldridge; Andrew Oldham; David Hockney; Edna O'Brien; Julie Christie; Lee Marvin; Michael Caine; and Mick Jagger. The Pink Floyd track is misspelled as above on sleeve and labels. Labels credit LP title as above whilst the sleeve misses out the apostrophe in "Let's". Lorrimer Films Ltd., which made the film, was Whitehead's company.

INLP 003 ***VARIOUS ARTISTS/OST: Gulliver's Travels***

Side 1	Side 2	
1. Intro	1. Gulliver Travels	**Rel:** 1969
2. The Journey	2. America	
3. Gulliver Travels	3. Afterglow	
4. The Sea	4. Laputa	

Withdrawn for contractual reasons – see IM 075 for further information. Includes snippets of music by the Small Faces, The Nice, Cosmic Sounds, Loving Spoonful and Little Richard. *Afterglow* is a lovely version of the Small Faces' song by Bob Kerr's Whoopee Band. Tracks above are as per labels, but side 1 has six distinct track bands, whilst side 2 has eight.

INSP 004 ***SAMSON: Are You Samson?***

Side 1	Side 2	
1. Traffic	1. Mars	**Rel:** Aug 1969[14]
2. Sleep	2. Venus	
3. Journey	3. Saturn	
4. Fair		
5. The End Song		

Rumoured to exist in mono, as INLP 004, though not confirmed. The summer 1969 release date and the fact that EMI's *Export Numerical Catalogue Service* listing does not mention a mono version (it does in all other instances) would tend to suggest that no mono version was issued.

IN sequence 7" singles

All singles were on orange labels and all are confirmed with die–cut, four–prong centres, except for IN 005, which is only confirmed with solid centre. IN 004 is confirmed with both types of centre. Singles came complete in company sleeves.

IN 001 ***OUTER LIMITS: Great Train Robbery/Sweet Freedom***

Rel: Sep 1968[14]

Originally intended for Immediate release,as IM 067, in May 1968. Demonstration copies were pressed before the release was put on hold. A P.P. Arnold single was released on IM 067 instead. This version is slightly different to that pressed on the Immediate label demo.

IN 002 ***THE EXELSIOR SPRING: Happy Miranda/It***

Rel: 6 Dec 1968[10/14]/3 Jan 1969[3]

Promotional copies have a large "A" and "DEMONSTRATION RECORD NOT FOR SALE" text. Promotional copies seem to be more numerous than stock copies.

IN 003 ***EDDIE THORNTON OUTFIT: Baby Be My Girl/SONNY BURKE OUTFIT: All You***

Rel: 24 Jan[3]/Jan 1969[14]

IN 004 ***COPPERFIELD: Any Old Time (You're Lonely And Sad)/I'm No Good For Her***

Rel: 20 Jun[10]/Jun[14]/4 Jul 1969[3]

Also confirmed with solid centre. Promotional copies with large "A" without "DEMONSTRATION" text. This was issued on the Immediate label in various other territories.

IN 005 ***TWINKLE: Micky/Darby And Joan***

Rel: Jul[14]/15 Aug 1969[3]

Only solid–centred copies confirmed.

REVOLUTION

Revolution was kicked off by Tony Calder in conjunction with Dave Hadfield as a subsidiary label to Instant rather than to Immediate. Many more records were released on the various Revolution labels (Rocksteady, Pop, Soul, Children's Series and Classics), but the following represent the only two issued whilst the label was associated with Instant/Immediate. Both singles were on yellow/black labels with "Rocksteady" sub–heading. Both records are confirmed with four–prong, die–cut centres.

REV sequence 7" singles

REV 001 ***OWEN GREY AND THE MAXIMUM BREED: Sitting In The Park/ PETE HUNT AND THE MAXIMUM BREED: You've Got It***

Rel: Mar 1969 (see below)
Included "A Dave Hadfield Production" and "Immediate Records Limited" credits on labels. Release date as listed on 45cat.com and may not be accurate.

REV 002 ***JIMMY SCOTT: Ob–La–Di Ob–La–Da Story Alullo (Part I)/Ob–La–Di Ob–La–Da Story Doh (Part II)***

Rel: 6 Dec[10]/3 Jan 1968[3]
The credits are a bit confused. The labels make it look as though the artist is "ALULLO (Part I)" on the a–side and "DOH (Part II) on the b–side, with Jimmy Scott's name only appearing in small text and in brackets. Both sides are published by Immediate Music but perhaps the writing was already on the wall with the "Immediate Records Limited" credit conspicuous by its absence. Promotional copies include a large "A" and release date, but no "DEMONSTRATION" text. Later reissued by Revolution on orange label design as REVS 505.

BANG REISSUES ROUND–UP

When it came to the reissue of McCoys material originally licensed by Immediate from Bang Records, I decided to break the rules about listing labels in order of first release and, instead, roll up all subsequent qualifying reissues in one place. Otherwise we would have three pages with little in the way of information. This information appears here because this, chronologically, is where the first McCoys reissue would appear.

Immediate ceased issuing new McCoys material in the UK following the release of *I Got To Go Back* (IM 046), which was one of the last records to be issued under the original Philips marketing agreement in early 1968; perhaps it was the change of distributor that was the driver for Lester Bangs to move elsewhere. After Immediate's move to EMI, new McCoys material was issued in the UK, first on Decca's London label, and then on Mercury. Once the group had broken up, back catalogue seems to have been licensed in piecemeal fashion until Bang set up its own UK label and included the pairing of its two only UK hits amongst its first set of otherwise contemporary releases.

The 1980 reissue of *Hang On Sloopy* (listed as Lightning, LR 8108) isn't included because, although listed in UK trade publications, it was an (US?) import. The Old Gold reissue (OG 9549) of the London/Bang coupling of the two UK hits isn't here either because it was reissued in September 1985, the month after this discography ends

Joy Label LP

JOYS 196 ***THE McCOYS: Hang On Sloopy***

See IMLP 001 for track listing

Rel: Jun 1971[1]
RRP: £1.30[1]
Del: 1974[5]

Flipback sleeve. The rear of the sleeve was markedly different to the Immediate release and had the cartoon girl from the front added in black and white along with photos of the band.

London label 7" single

HML 10480 ***THE McCOYS: Hang On Sloopy/Fever***

Rel: 28 Feb 1975[3]

Includes the Bang Records logo on labels. Stock copies on the usual black label design with silver text; demos on red label design with silver text.

Bang label 7" single

BANG 003 ***THE McCOYS: Hang On Sloopy/Fever***

Rel: 29 Oct 1976[3]

Pressed by Phonogram with moulded plastic labels. Some copies have gold coloured labels whilst others are silver.

NEW WORLD

The budget New World label seems to have been the first UK label to spot the potential of reissuing Immediate back catalogue (Bang Records material notwithstanding) and an LP appeared in 1972 with what seems to be a mix of Deram and Immediate–era tracks by Amen Corner and Decca–era recordings by the Small Faces (even if some of the tracks had appeared on Immediate on *The Autumn Stone* in 1969).

There was another LP, NW 6000, by the Small Faces, which comprised purely Decca–era recordings, so that's not documented here (even if some might have been Immediate Productions recordings that had been licensed to Decca). As for provenance, there's no clue on either labels or sleeves, so who licensed these recordings – if indeed anyone licensed them – remains an unknown. The album enjoyed a much longer life than did the original groups and was available until around 1979 by the look of things.

New World seems to have had a bit of a thing about truncating long song titles (even more so on the Small Faces LP). The titles below are as credited on sleeve and labels.

New World LP

NW 6001 **AMEN CORNER AND SMALL FACES: *Amen Corner And Small Faces***

Side 1: Small Faces	*Side 2: Amen Corner*	**Rel:** 1972
1. Shake	1. High In The Sky	**RRP:** 87p[4]
2. Come On Children	2. Cocaine Blues	
3. Sha La La La Lee	3. *Things Ain't What*	
4. My Mind's Eye	4. *Evil Man's Gonna Win*	
5. Watcha Gonna Do	5. *Hey Hey Girl*	
6. Hey Girl	6. Run Run Run	
7. Runaway	7. *Half As Nice*	

Original label design black with 1972 publication date. Later copies appeared on various other colour labels. Sleeve credits artists as above whilst labels credit "Small Faces/Amen Corner". The Small Faces get side 1, so I suppose that they win on points. The Immediate–era tracks are italicised, though this is based on the assumptions that all tracks are studio recordings – any live versions would be Immediate recordings – and that they are the same versions as released previously. *Things Ain't What* should be *Things Ain't What The Used To Be. Cocaine Blues* is also an Immediate–era recording, though unreleased at the time, and exists on a one–sided Emidisc acetate (complete with interesting, hand–written spellings). The track listing on the acetate is: *Mr Nonchelant*; *Cociane Blues*; *The Hustler*, *Lady Riga*; *Stop And Get A Hold Of Yourself*, *Thing Ain't What They Used To Be*. Tracks 3 and 5 from the acetate, along with the aforementioned track 2, were not issued by Immediate.

CHARLY

These records were issued during 1975/76 and appeared on the CR 300000 (FC) catalogue series, which was started in 1974. Gaps in the sequence below relate to non–Immediate back catalogue releases. No distinction was made between single and double albums in the sequence. The records were on the Charly label design with the Immediate logo on the rear sleeve only. Records were manufactured and distributed by Pye Records (Sales) Ltd, licensed from Oldham's US–based Immediate Records Inc. Whilst other Charly releases around this time were advised to trade publications, none of the following seem to have been advised at time of release, though all were freely available in the UK.

Charly LPs

CR 300014 (FC) THE NICE: Nice

See IMSP 026 for track listing **Rel:** 1975

Straight reissue in new sleeve design, which includes the sub–credit "Featuring Keith Emerson, Lee Jackson, Brian Davison".

CR 300015 (FC) SMALL FACES: Ogden's Nut Gone Flake

See IMSP 012 for track listing **Rel:** 1975

Reissue of the stereo version in square, single sleeve design.

CR 300016 (FC) Humble Pie: Town And Country

See IMSP 012 for track listing **Rel:** 1975

New sleeve design. This UK issue was later listed in trade listings as a French import with release date of August 1978, RRP of £3.25 and notification of deletion (presumably during 1983)[6].

CR 300017 (FC) VARIOUS ARTISTS: Bastards Of British Rock (2–LP)

Rel: 1975

Record 1: side 1

1. On Top Of The World (John Mayall And The Bluesbreakers With Eric Clapton)
2. Man Of The World (Fleetwood Mac)
3. Water On My Fire (Albert Lee And Paul Williams)
4. Handbags And Gladrags (Chris Farlowe)
5. Piano Shuffle (The All Stars Featuring Nicky Hopkins)
6. Gin House (Amen Corner)
7. Itchyocoo Park (Small Faces)

Record 1: side 2

1. Little Miss Understood (Rod Stewart)
2. Tribute To Elmore (Eric Clapton And Jimmy Page)
3. Brandenburger (The Nice)
4. When You Got A Good Friend (Tony McPhee)
5. Steelin' (Jeff Beck And The All Stars)
6. Cold Lady (Humble Pie)
7. Azrael Revisited (The Nice)

Record 2: side 1
1. Telephone Blues (John Mayall And The Bluesbreakers)
2. Can't Quit You Baby (Savoy Brown Blues Band)
3. Who's Knocking (Jeremy Spencer)
4. My Way Of Giving (Chris Farlowe)
5. Miles Road (Eric Clapton And Jimmy Page)
6. Lazy Sunday (Small Faces)
7. Down To The Boots (The All Stars Featuring Jimmy Page)

Record 2: side 2
1. So Much To Say (Rod Stewart)
2. America (The Nice)
3. Cold Blooded Woman (Savoy Brown Blues Band)
4. West Coast Idea (Eric Clapton)
5. Alabama 69 (Humble Pie)
6. Chuckles (Jeff Beck And The All Stars)
7. I'm Your Witchdoctor (John Mayall And The Bluesbreakers)

Released in various other territories as *Rock Roots*.

CR 300019 (FC) THE NICE: Ars Longa Vita Brevis

See IMSP 020 for track listing **Rel:** 1975

New sleeve design, which includes the sub–credit "Featuring Keith Emerson, Lee Jackson, Brian Davison".

CR 300020 (FC) CHRIS FARLOWE: Out Of Time – Paint It Black

Rel: 1976

1. Paint It Black
2. Yesterday's Papers
3. Everyone Makes A Mistake
4. Moanin'
5. Out Of Time

1. Ride On Baby
2. Headlines
3. What Have I Been Doing
4. My Way Of Giving
5. Handbags And Gladrags

Listed as a 1978 release French import[5], though it is confirmed that UK copies existed prior to 1978.

CR 300021 (FC) THE NICE: The Thoughts Of Emerlist Davjack

See IMSP 016 for track listing **Rel:** 1976

Reissue of the stereo version in new sleeve design, which includes the sub–credit "Keith Emerson, Lee Jackson, Brian Davison & David O'List".

CR 300025 (FC) SMALL FACES: The Autumn Stone (2–LP)

See IMAL 01/02 for track listing **Rel:** 1975

New (and awful) sleeve design. Front of sleeve does not include the album title. Listed as a French import with title *The Small Faces Live U.K. 1969*[5] – *The Record Collector Rare Record Guide 2012* states that this is a UK–manufactured export LP, under the same title. It is perfectly possible that copies for export included a sticker with this text though, if so, it would be misleading because less than a quarter of the LP is recorded live (and at the wrong speed). Release date of August 1978 with RRP of £4.98 listed[5], though the album was definitely available in the UK in 1975.

NEMS/IMMEDIATE

NEMS Immediate reissues were originally manufactured by CBS (distributed by Anchor for the first single), following which they moved to RCA for manufacturing, followed by Pye. There was then a brief hiatus during which NEMS material was licensed to Virgin for release before NEMS moved to Stage One for manufacture. It looks as though cassette versions changed catalogue prefixes during the move to Stage One distribution – and it looks as though at least one pre–existing album was issued on cassette only after the move to Stage One, though trade publications were not advised.

A new catalogue sequence appeared in 1981 with NEMS logo adorning the white Immediate label design, just like the previous NEMS/Immediate IMS 100 series (the "S" in all cases denoting 'stereo'). This was short–lived and in 1982 selected singles were reissued on their original Immediate catalogue numbers (though stereo where stereo versions existed); on all bar IM 064 NEMS credits were conspicuous by their absence.

In the middle of this series of reissues, a one–off sequence was started when a Chris Farlowe single appeared as IMS 201, though it was packaged as though part of the IM 000 reissue series. Just to add some extra confusion, as from late 1982 all new NEMS releases and re–pressings included the credit "Issued under Licence to Pablocrown Ltd." as did all new pressings of NEMS/Immediate LPs and cassettes. This was replaced by a Zeema Productions marketing credit in (probably) 1983. That these were NEMS spin–off companies is likely, but not confirmed.

All Immediate–branded issues on NEMS included a bright, white Immediate label design, most with NEMS logo on labels and sleeves. The few exceptions are documented in the following listings. Singles were mostly issued with solid centres; again, exceptions are documented on a per record basis.

It is possible that some of the unused catalogue numbers relate to proposed new Immediate material from Marianne Faithfull (and, possibly, intriguingly, Black Sabbath). However, these were issued on the NEMS label proper and not on Immediate as originally planned in 1974. This was 'rectified' later, during yet another relaunch of Immediate, this time by both Andrew Oldham and Tony Calder in the US in 1994, when Marianne Faithfull appeared (along with Yardbirds material previously released by Charly) on promotional materials alongside the more usual Immediate suspects.

IMS 100 sequence 7" singles

IMS 101 ***CHRIS FARLOWE: Out Of Time/My Way Of Giving***

Rel: 19 Sep 1975[3] **Del:** 1977[5]/1978[9]

No NEMS logo on labels, but there is a "Marketed by NEMS Records" credit, though in a different place to that on subsequent issues in the series. Listed as "Immediate/Anchor/CBS" distribution[8]. Number 44 in the UK charts.

IMS 102 ***SMALL FACES: Itchycoo Park/My Way Of Giving***

Rel: 28 Nov 1975[3] (del Dec 1978[9])

Also exists with four–prong, die–cut centre. NEMS logo on labels. Listed as "Immediate/Nems/CBS" distribution[8]. *The New Singles* lists the b–side, erroneously, as *My Mind's Eye*.

IMS 103 ***AMEN CORNER FEATURING ANDY FAIRWEATHER LOW: (If Paradise Is) Half As Nice/When We Make Love***

Rel: Jan[5]/6 Feb[3]/14 Feb 1976[9] (del :1978[5])

The "featuring ANDY FAIRWEATHER LOW" part is printed in smaller point size under main artist credit. Both sides include the further subcredit, "(From the LP "The Return Of The Magnificent Seven" – IML 1004)". Promotional copies have a medium–sized "A" on the a–side label and "NOT FOR SALE" on both labels. Listed as "Immediate/Nems/CBS" distribution[5].

IMS 104 ***NO RELEASE LISTED***

IMS 105 ***HUMBLE PIE: Natural Born Woman/I'll Go Alone (UNISSUED?)***

Rel: see below

Release unconfirmed though listed with February 1976 release date with a–side title as above[5]. 45cat.com lists this as "Natural Born Bugie" coupled with "I'll Go Alone" but, tellingly, there is no label photo. Not listed in *The New Singles*.

IMS 106 ***SMALL FACES: Lazy Sunday/(Tell Me) Have You Ever Seen Me***

Rel: 19 Mar 1976[3] (del: Mar 1979[9])

The a–side includes the subcredit, "(From the Immediate L.P. "Ogdens Nutgone Flake" – IML 1001)" though a demo version exists without this credit.

IMS 107 ***CRISPIAN ST. PETERS: You Were On My Mind/TRAXTER: Glandular Fever***

Rel: 28 May 1976[3]

NEMS logo on labels. Listed as "Immediate/Nems/CBS" distribution[5]. Labels include the text, "An Original Immediate Recording" even though neither side was. The b–side seems to be the backing track for Donovan's *Hey Gyp (Dig the Slowness)* as released on Deram by The Truth (DM 105). On the Deram single, Donovan gets the writing credit (as you would expect) with David Nicholson credited as producer. On this release Nicholson gets writing and production credits. Promotional copies have a medium–sized "A" on the a–side label and "NOT FOR SALE" on both labels.

IMS 108 ***NO RELEASE LISTED***

IMS 109 ***P. P. ARNOLD: The First Cut Is The Deepest/THE IMMEDIATE ALL–STARS: King Of Kings***

Rel: 20 May 1977[3] (del: 1978[5])

The b–side does not include the "An Original Immediate Recording" text, so where did this recording originate? Promotional copies have a medium–sized "A" on the a–side label and "NOT FOR SALE" on both labels. Listed as "Immediate/Nems/RCA" distribution[8]. Curiously, Barry Green (curator of the Immediate archive at Charly) has a four–prong, die–cut copy with a 7 Aug 1976 date stamp.

IMS 110 ***SMALL FACES: Tin Soldier/I Feel Much Better***

Rel: 20 May 1977[3]

This only seems to exist with four–prong, die–cut centre. A–side label includes, "From "The Best of the Small Faces" IML 2008." All well and good, but the LP did not see release for quite a while after this and was titled *Small Faces' Greatest Hits* by the time it was released. Listed as "Immediate/Nems/RCA" distribution[5].

IML 1000 sequence LPs

The following LPs are all listed in *Music Master* (IML 1001 in the 2nd Edition and the rest in the 5th Edition) with "Immediate/Nems/CBS" distribution credits.

IML 1001 SMALL FACES: Ogden's Nut Gone Flake

See IMSP 012 for track listing		**Rel:** Dec 1975[4]/ Jan 1976[1]
		RRP: £2.99[1]

Cassette: IMC 1001 — **Rel:** Jan 1976[2] — **RRP:** £2.99[2]

Reissue of the stereo version in circular, fold–out sleeve. White label test pressings in plain white sleeve exist, though these may be for the later IML 2001 release, thinking about it.

IML 1002 CHRIS FARLOWE: Out Of Time

1. Out Of Time	1. Handbags And Gladbags	**Rel:** Dec 1975[4/5]/ Jan 1976[1]
2. The Last Goodbye	2. Reach Out I'll Be There	
3. Ride On Baby	3. Moanin'	**RRP:** £2.99[1]
4. My Way Of Giving	4. Yesterday's Papers	
5. Think	5. Dawn	
6. Satisfaction	6. Paint It Black	

Cassette: IMC 1002 — **Rel:** Jan 1976[2] — **RRP:** £2.99[2]

IML 1003 THE NICE: Amoeni Redivivi

1. Rondo	1a. America (From 'West Side Story')	**Rel:** Mar 1976[5] Apr 1976[1]
2. Hang On To A Dream	1b. Second Amendment	
3. The Thoughts Of Emerlist Davjack	2. The Cry Of Eugene	**RRP:** £2.79[1] £2.99[5]
4. Intermezzo From The Karelia Suite	3. The Diamond Hard Apples Of The Moon	
	4. Ars Longa Vita Brevis 3rd Movement: Acceptence 'Brandenburger'	
	5. Ars Longa Vita Brevis 4th Movement: Denial	

Cassette: IMC 1003 — **Rel:** not advised — **RRP:** pres. £2.99

8–track cartridge : IMT 1003 — **Rel:** not advised — **RRP:** pres. £2.99

Track 3, side 2 misses "Blue" on label but sleeve includes full credit. Tracks 1a and 4, side 2 have single speech marks on labels but double speech marks on sleeve. Tape versions are listed on the LP sleeve, but neither seem to have been advised to trade publications.

IML 1004 AMEN CORNER: Return Of The Magnificent Seven

1. (If Paradise Is) Half As Nice	1. At Last I've Found Someone To Love	**Rel:** Mar 1976[5]/ Apr 1976[1]
2. Hello Susie	2. Proud Mary	**RRP:** £2.79[1]/ £2.99[5]
3. The Weight	3. Penny Lane (Live Version)	
4. When We Make Love	4. High In The Sky (Live Version)	
5. Get Back	5. Gin House (Live Version)	
	6. Bend Me, Shape Me (Live Version)	

Cassette: IMC 1004 — **Rel:** not advised — **RRP:** pres. £2.99

Sleeve includes subcredit, "Featuring Andy Fair–weather Low". Cassette has *Penny Lane* and *At Last I've Found Someone To Love* as tracks A4 and A5. On side 2 only the last two tracks remain in the same position as on the LP with *High In The Sky*, *When We Make Love*, *Proud Mary* and *Get Back* in that order before them. Cassette also includes the "(Live Version)" credits.

IML 1005 ***HUMBLE PIE: Back Home Again***

1. Natural Born Woman	1. The Sad Bag Of Shaky Jake	**Rel:** Jul 1976[5]
2. Desperation	2. Home And Away	**RRP:** £2.99[5]
3. A Nifty Little Number Like You	3. Heartbeat	
4. Every Mother's Son	4. Silver Tongue	
5. Alabama '69	5. As Safe As Yesterday	
	6. Down Home Again	

Natural Born Bugie miscredited on both sleeve and label as "Natural Born Woman". LP later reissued in new sleeve design as "Humble Pie's Greatest Hits" (IML 2005) despite including just the one hit.

IML 1006 ***NO RELEASE LISTED***

IML 1007 ***NO RELEASE LISTED***

Note that rumours of P.P. Arnold's *Kafunta* on this catalogue number appear to relate to the original South African release from 1969.

IML 1008 ***SMALL FACES: Magic Moments***

1. Itchycoo Park	1. Lazy Sunday	**Rel:** Jul 1976[5]
2. I Can't Make It	2. Just Passing	**RRP:** £2.99[5]
3. Green Circles	3. Wham Bam Thank You Mam	
4. The Universal	4. My Way O Giving	
5. Wide Eyed Girl	5. Afterglow (Of Your Love)	
6. Here Come The Nice	6. Tin Soldier	

Is my memory wandering or is *Green Circles* a slightly different version to that usually heard? Track 3, side 2 has changed sex since the original single label credit – "Mam" instead of "Man".

IML 2000 sequence LPs

Apart from IML 2001, this sequence concentrated on well–padded 'Greatest Hits' packages. One wonders what was intended for IML 2007 because all of the usual suspects are accounted for. The following are all listed with "Immediate/Nems/Pye" distribution[5] except for IML 2001, which is listed as "Immediate/Nems/ RCA".

IML 2001 ***SMALL FACES: Ogden's Nut Gone Flake***

See IMSP 012 for track listing

Rel: Jun[5]/Jul '77[1]
RRP: £3.49[1/5]
Del: 1978[5]

Cassette: IMK 2001 **Rel:** Jun[5]/Jul 1977[1] (del: 1978[5]) **RRP:** £3.50[1/5]

Round sleeve. Reissued with a different catalogue number for reasons probably related to change of distributor. See IML 1001 for information on white label test pressing.

IML 2002 ***CHRIS FARLOWE: Greatest Hits***

1. (I Can't Get No) Satisfaction	1. Paint It Black	**Rel:** Jan 1978[1/5]
2. Ride On Baby	2. Yesterday's Papers	**RRP:** £3.75[1/5]
3. What Becomes Of The Broken Hearted	3. In the Midnight Hour	
4. The Fool	4. Reach Out I'll Be There	
5. Think	5. Moaning	
6. Handbags And Gladrags	6. Out Of Time	

Track A3 credited as "What Became of the Broken Hearted" on first release, IMLP/IMSP 006.

IML 2003 *THE NICE: Greatest Hits*

1. Medley:
   a. America (Adpt. From "West Side Story")
   b. 2nd Amendment
2. Hang On To A Dream
3. Intermezzo (From Karelia Suite)

1. The Thoughts Of Emerlist Davjack
2. The Diamond Hard Blue Apples Of The Moon
3. The Cry Of Eugene
4. Rondo
5. Ars Longa Vita Brevis (3rd Movement) Acceptance Brandenburger
6. Ars Longa Vita Brevis (4th Movement) Denial

Rel: Jan 1978[1/5]
RRP: £3.75[1/5]
Del: 1978[5]

Cassette: ZCIM 2003 **Rel:** Jan. 1978[1/5] **RRP:** £4.05[1]

The European compilation finally appeared in the UK. Track listing above as credited on labels: sleeve does not include "Medley" credit for track 1, but credits track as having two parts ("Adapted" also appears in full); track 4, side 1 credited as "from the Karelia Suite" on sleeve (no brackets); "Blue" missing from track 2, side 2 on sleeve. Later (probably 1983) copies, with records credited as being made in Eire, have updated sleeve design (though just to confuse issues sleeve has a "Made in England" credit along with "Issued under licence to Zeema Records Ltd." credit). *Music Master* lists cassette RRP as £3.75[5].

IML 2004 *AMEN CORNER: Amen Corner's Greatest Hits Featuring Andy Fairweather Low*

1. (If Paradise Is) Half As Nice
2. Get Back
3. Lady Riga
4. The Weight
5. When We Make Love
6. Recess

1. Hello Susie
2. At Last I've Found Someone To Love
3. So Fine (Live)
4. High In The Sky (Live)
5. Gin House Blues (Live)
6. Bend Me, Shape Me (Live)

Rel: Jan 1978[1/5]
RRP: £3.75[1/5]

Cassette: IMC 2004 (if it exists; see below)

Title as credited on labels, otherwise sleeve shows title as "Greatest Hits" with "featuring Andy Fairweather Low" as subcredit. Spine credits title as "Amen Corner's Greatest Hits". Track 5, side 2 credited as "Gin House (Live)" on sleeve, missing out "Blues". 1980s cassette issue probably exists, though, if so, not advised to trade publications.

IML 2005 *HUMBLE PIE FEATURING PETER FRAMPTON AND STEVE MARRIOTT: Humble Pie's Greatest Hits*

1. Natural Born Bugie
2. Desperation
3. A Nifty Little Number Like You
4. Every Mother's Son
5. Alabama '69

1. The Sad Bag Of Shaky Jake
2. Home And Away
3. Heartbeat
4. Silver Tongue
5. As Safe As Yesterday
6. Down Home Again

Rel: Jan 1978[1/5]
RRP: £3.75[1/5]
Del: 1978[5]

Cassette: ZCIM 2005 **Rel:** Jan. 1978[1/5] **RRP:** £4.05[1]
Cassette: IMC 2005 **Rel:** 1980s

Front sleeve credits "Humble Pie Greatest Hits" with "featuring Peter Frampton Steve Marriott Jerry Shirley Greg Ridley" (no punctuation) as subtitle; spine and label credits as above. *Natural Born Bugie* miscredited on sleeve as "Natural Born Woman", but correctly credited on label. 1977 publication date on labels. Straight reissue of *Back Home Again* compilation from 1976 (IML 1005) – track listing included because of the altered credit for track 1, side 1. *Music Master* lists cassette RRP as £3.75[5].

IML 2006 ***P. P. ARNOLD: Greatest Hits***

Side 1	Side 2	
1. The First Cut Is The Deepest	1. Angel Of The Morning	**Rel:** Jan 1978[1/5]
2. Dreaming	2. As Tears Go By	**RRP:** £3.75[1/5]
3. Would You Believe	3. Am I Still Dreaming	
4. To Love Somebody	4. Though Its Hurt Me Badly	
5. Born To Be Together	5. Speak To Me	
6. Eleanor Rigby	6. (If You Think You're) Groovy	

Cassette: IMC 2006 **Rel:** 1980s

Track 4, side 2 as listed on record but should be "Though It Hurts Me Badly". Side 2 matrix in run–off was originally a handwritten "IMS–2006–B" with the "S" crossed out and "L" added above. White label test pressings in plain white sleeve exist. Cassette issue confirmed only with Pablocrown credits; it certainly doesn't seem to have been issued on cassette on first release and the guess is that the cassette was only issued after the move to Stage One distribution.

IML 2007 ***NO RELEASE LISTED***

It is possible that this catalogue number was intended for Marianne Faithfull's *Dreamin' My Dreams*. It might, instead, have been intended for *Black Sabbath's Greatest Hits*. Perhaps the Black Sabbath LP is more likely because every other IML 2000 series release (except for IML 2001) is a greatest hits package and all (again bar IML 2001) were issued this same month (as were the Black Sabbath and Marianne Faithfull LPs). You pays your money and you takes your choice.

IML 2008 ***SMALL FACES: Small Faces' Greatest Hits***

Side 1	Side 2	
1. Itchycoo Park	1. Tin Soldier	**Rel:** Jan 1978[1/5]
2. Wham Bam Thank You Mam	2. Autumn Stone	**RRP:** £3.75[1/5]
3. The Universal	3. Afterglow	
4. Son Of A Baker	4. Red Balloon	
5. René	5. All Or Nothing (Live)	
6. Here Comes The Nice	6. Lazy Sunday	

Cassette: ZCIM 2008 **Rel:** Jan 1978[1/5] **RRP:** £4.05[1]

No apostrophe in album title on labels. Track 2, side 1 says "Mam" (original single is "Man"). The last track on side 1 says "Comes" (original single is "Come"). "Afterglow" does not include "(Of Your Love)" and, although appearing as above on label, is credited as "AFTER GLOW" on sleeve. Labels include 1977 publication date.

IMS 700 sequence 7" singles

The label is the usual bright, white Immediate design and both have solid centres. Both records include the NEMS logo.

IMS 701 ***SMALL FACES: Lazy Sunday/Autumn Stone***

Rel: Sep 1981[6]

Listed as "Immediate/Immediate/Stage One" distribution[6].

IMS 702 ***HUMBLE PIE: Natural Born Bugie/Alabama '69***

Rel: Sep 1981[8]

IM reissue sequence 7" singles

All of the following, bar IM 064, were conspicuous by the absence of NEMS logo and credits on labels or sleeves, though early releases were listed with NEMS distribution. Later pressings from 1983 include "Issued under licence to Pablocrown Ltd." text. All labels are bright, white Immediate label designs and all records have solid centres. These seem to be stereo versions hence some credited in trade listings as IMS?

IM 003 ***NICO: I'm Not Sayin'/The Last Mile***
Rel: 14 May[1]/2 Jul 1982[1]
Picture sleeve. Listed as "IMS 003"[6] but copies confirmed as "IM 003". Listed as "Immediate/Immediate/Stage One" distribution[6].

IM 047 ***P.P. ARNOLD: First Cut Is The Deepest/Speak To Me***
Rel: 24 Dec 1982[1]
Picture sleeve. This reissue misses "The" from the start of the a–side title on label and sleeve. Listed as "IMS 047"[6] but most likely "IM 047". Listed as "Immediate/Immediate/Stage One" distribution[6].

IM 060 ***ROD STEWART: Little Miss Understood/So Much To Say***
Rel: Apr 1982[8]/Feb 1983[6]
Picture sleeve. Labels include the credit "Issued under Licence to Pablocrown Ltd." Earlier release date listed as "Immediate/Nems/Stage One" distribution[8] whilst later release date listed as "Immediate/Immediate/Stage One" distribution[6/8]. I would imagine that any April 1982 copies, if it was issued at this point, would not include the Pablocrown credit.

IM 064 ***SMALL FACES: Lazy Sunday/Rollin' Over***
Rel: 29 Oct 1982[1] **Del:** Oct 1985[9]
Picture sleeve. NEMS logo on labels. Listed as "Immediate/Immediate/Stage One" distribution[6].

IM 067 ***P.P. ARNOLD: Angel Of The Morning/Life Is But Nothing***
Rel: Apr 1982[6]
Listed as "Immediate/Nems/Stage One" distribution[6]. However, was this really released?

IM 068 ***THE NICE: America (Adapted From West Side Story)/The Diamond Hard Apples Of The Moon***
Rel: 24 Dec 1982[1]
Picture sleeve. The b–side title misses out "Blue" from the title, as did the later pink label copies on the original Immediate label. Listed as "IMS 068"[6] but copies confirmed as "IM 068". Listed as "Immediate/Immediate/Stage One" distribution[8].

IM 080 ***FLEETWOOD MAC: Man Of The World/EARL VINCE AND THE VALIANTS: Somebody's Gonna Get Their Head Kicked In Tonite***
Rel: Feb 1983[6]
Picture sleeve. Labels include the credit "Issued under Licence to Pablocrown Ltd." Listed as "Immediate/Immediate/Stage One" distribution[6].

IM 082 ***HUMBLE PIE: Natural Born Bugie/Wrist Job***
Rel: Apr 1982[8]/Feb 1983[6]
Picture sleeve. Labels include the credit "Issued under Licence to Pablocrown Ltd." Earlier release date listed as "Immediate/Nems/Stage One" distribution[8] whilst later release date listed as "Immediate/Immediate/Stage One" distribution[6/8]. I would imagine that any April 1982 copies, if it was issued at this point, which is doubtful, would not include the Pablocrown credit.

IMS 200 sequence 7" single

Quite why a new catalogue sequence was started for just this one single is unknown, though presumably the "S" denoted a stereo issue. The picture sleeve was of the same design as the IM reissue series and, apart from the catalogue number, it looks to be a part of that series. The label is the usual bright, white Immediate design and all copies have solid centres.

IMS 201 CHRIS FARLOWE: Out Of Time/My Way Of Giving
Rel: Oct[5]/5 Nov 1982[1]
Picture sleeve. Listed as "Immediate/(Reissue)/Stage One" distribution[6].

IMLD sequence double LP

IMLD 01 ***SMALL FACES: Autumn Stone***

See IMAL 01/02 for track listing

Rel: Jul 1984[7]
RRP: £4.85[7]

Labels include "Issued under licence to Zeema Records Ltd" credit. Listed as "Immediate/Nems/Stage One" distribution[7].

Promotional sampler LP

NS 1 ***VARIOUS ARTISTS: Gems from NEMS***

Dist: 1980

1. Hello Suzie (Amen Corner)
2. *I Shot The Sheriff (Pluto)*
3. Tin Soldier (Small Faces)
4. America (The Nice)
5. *Paranoid (Black Sabbath)*

1. Handbags And Gladrags (Chris Farlowe)
2. *Signal Injector (Edgar Broughton Band)*
3. *Oh But If I (Tinga Stewart)*
4. Rene (Small Faces)
5. Natural Born Woman (Humble Pie)

Non–Immediate tracks in italic. Promotional record with Immediate, NEMS and Opal logos on sleeve. Sleeve includes credits, "Limited edition" and "For promotional use only". Perhaps this explains how Black Sabbath's *Paranoid* appeared as an Immediate–branded release in Europe via Ariola (not just once, but twice) in the early 1980s.

VIRGIN/NEMS

All Immediate catalogue material released by Virgin included "Licensed from NEMS Records" credits on either sleeves, labels or both (except, possibly, for V 2159 – see below). Apart from the SV 100 sequence set of doublepack EPs, all releases were on the Immediate label design with either bright white or pink backgrounds (and one blue label). All labels included Virgin logo and NEMS licensing credit.

V 2000 sequence LPs

V 2159 ***SMALL FACES: Ogden's Nut Gone Flake***

See IMLP/IMSP 012 for track listing

Rel: Mar[5]/Apr '80[1]
Lbl: white
RRP: £5.49[1]

Cassette: not issued[6]

Limited edition, circular, fold–out sleeve. Later copies in normal, square sleeve? Labels include the credit, "Re–released by Virgin Records" (all in upper case) under the Immediate logo. There is no mention of NEMS on labels and the circular–sleeved copy may not have included NEMS sleeve credits either. The side 2 matrix follows usual Virgin format ("V–2159 B3") on all copies but side 1 matrix is "C V–215–A3E" on at least some copies – others have a more usual "V 2159-A".

V 2165 ***VARIOUS ARTISTS: The Immediate Story***

1. Hang On Sloopy (The McCoys)
2. Here Comes The Nice (Small Faces)
3. America (The Nice)
4. You Baby (The Turtles)
5. Cara–Lin (Strangeloves)
6. (If Paradise Is) Half As Nice (Amen Corner)
7. Little Miss Understood (Rod Stewart)
8. The First Cut Is The Deepest (P.P. Arnold)

1. Out Of Time (Chris Farlowe)
2. Natural Born Bugie (Humble Pie)
3. I'm Your Witchdoctor (John Mayall's Bluesbreakers)
4. Man Of The World (Fleetwood Mac)
5. So Much In Love (Charles Dickens)
6. Sittin' On A Fence (Twice As Much)
7. I'm Not Saying (Nico)
8. I'm So Confused (Mick Softley)
9. That's Heaven To Me (Sam Cooke)

Rel: Jun 1980[6]
RRP: £3.99

Cassette: not issued[6]

Original release included a £3.99 "Special Price" sticker. Small Faces track credited as "Comes" (original single is "Come"). *America* does not include any sub–credits. P.P. Arnold track preceded by "The" on label but not on sleeve. The artist for *I'm Your Witchdoctor* is credited as above on label but as "John Mayall and the Bluesbreakers" on the sleeve. Hm, funny, but the Turtles, Strangeloves and Sam Cooke tracks included on this album were most likely not owned by NEMS at the time, having only been licensed to Immediate. Don't tell anyone.

V 2166 ***SMALL FACES: Big Hits***

1. Watcha Gonna Do 'Bout It
2. I've Got Mine
3. Sha La La La Lee
4. Hey Girl
5. All Or Nothing
6. My Mind's Eye
7. I Can't Make It

1. Here Comes The Nice
2. Itchycoo Park
3. Tin Soldier
4. Lazy Sunday
5. The Universal
6. Afterglow (Of Your Love)
7. Wham Bam Thank You Mam

Rel: Jul[5]/Sep '80[1]
Lbl: white
RRP: £5.29[1]

Cassette: TCV 2166 (Jul. 1980[6])
Limited edition gatefold sleeve, later copies in single sleeve. Side 1 and *Tin Soldier* mono. Track 1, side 2 credited as "Comes" (original single is "Come") and track 7, side 2 credited as "Mam" (original single is "Man"). Sleeve claims "All the hit singles – original versions!" but if the Decca–era tracks are the original single versions, were these also owned by NEMS?

V 2176 ***VARIOUS ARTISTS: Immediate Blues***

1. Water On My Fire (Albert Lee)
2. Steelin (Jeff Beck)
3. Draggin My Tail (Eric Clapton/ Jimmy Page)
4. The Next Milestone (Albert Lee)
5. Snakedrive (Eric Clapton)
6. On Top Of The World (John Mayall)

1. Telephone Blues (John Mayall)
2. Choker (Eric Clapton/Jimmy Page)
3. Chuckles (Jeff Beck)
4. Tribute To Elmore (Eric Clapton)
5. Crosstown Link (Albert Lee)
6. West Coast Idea (Eric Clapton/ Jimmy Page)

Rel: 1980
Lbl: blue

Artist credits as per labels. Tracks 2 and 3, side 1, both have apostrophes in appropriate place on sleeve but not on labels. Most artist credits differ as well with sleeve crediting "John Mayall's Bluesbreakers", "All Stars featuring Jeff Beck" and "Eric Clapton with Jimmy Page". Label colour is blue. Ah, a visual joke.

V 2178 ***SMALL FACES: For Your Delight, The Darlings of Whapping Wharf Launderette***

1. Talk To You
2. Feeling Lonely
3. Don't Burst My Bubble
4. Things Are Going To Get Better
5. My Way Of Giving
6. Runaway

1. (Tell Me) Have You Ever Seen Me
2. Up The Wooden Hills To Bedfordshire
3. Become Like You
4. Green Circles
5. Show Me The Way
6. All Our Yesterdays

Rel: Oct 1980[6]
Lbl: pink

Cassette: not issued[6]
Side 1, tracks 1 and 3, mono.

SV sequence doublepack 7" EPs

The records below were on a custom label design with "The Immediate catalogue" on both gatefold sleeves and labels – each was the same design though with different colour rectangular blocks under the heading. Sleeves and labels both included NEMS and Virgin logos and did not include the Immediate logo. Note that SV 101 did not include Immediate material (*Teeth* by The Mekons).

SV 102 CHRIS FARLOWE: The Immediate Catalogue: Out Of Time

Record 1: side 1
1. Out Of Time

Record 1: side 2
1. Yesterday's Papers
2. Ride On Baby

Rel: Jun 1980[6]
RRP: £1.75

Record 2: side 1	*Record 2: side 2*
1. Handbags And Gladrags	1. Paint It Black

Sleeve sticker includes RRP of £1.75. Red, rectangular blocks on sleeve and labels.

SV 103 P. P. ARNOLD: The Immediate Catalogue: Angel Of The Morning

Record 1: side 1	*Record 1: side 2*	**Rel:** 1980
1. Angel Of The Morning	1. Everything's Gonna Be Alright	**RRP:** £1.75
Record 2: side 1	*Record 2: side 2*	
1. The First Cut Is The Deepest	1. (If You Think You're) Groovy	
	2. The Time Has Come	

Sleeve sticker includes RRP £1.75. Blue, rectangular blocks on sleeve and labels.

SV 104 AMEN CORNER: The Immediate Catalogue: (If Paradise Is) Half As Nice

Record 1: side 1	*Record 1: side 2*	**Rel:** 27 Jun '80[1]
1. (If Paradise Is) Half As Nice	1. Hello Susie	**Del:** 1980[6]
Record 2: side 1	*Record 2: side 2*	
1. Bend Me Shape Me (Live)	1. Gin House Blues (Live)	
	2. High In The Sky (Live)	

All copies viewed so far have been very obviously sticker free, which is not to say that it did not include one. Green, rectangular blocks on sleeve and labels. Sleeve notes claim erroneously that *(If Paradise Is) Half As Nice* was Immediate's first number one single in the UK. So what do the Chris Farlowe sleeve notes say then? Ah, they say that *Out Of Time* was number one, only earlier. Who'd be a sleeve notes writer?

VS sequence 7" singles

The two singles below were issued on bright white Immediate label design with NEMS licensing credits.

Various assertions that the April 1980[6] Crispian St. Peters coupling of *You Were On My Mind / Pied Piper* was either released by Immediate or that it was released by Virgin on an Immediate label design are erroneous. It was licensed from NEMS but was issued on the then current Virgin label design. The confusion stems from the fact that the 1984 edition of *Music Master* fails to list it as a Virgin release and instead includes the incorrect distribution path, "Immediate/CBS/CBS".

VS 366 ROD STEWART: Little Miss Understood/So Much To Say

Rel: 1980

Picture sleeve. Only solid–centred copies confirmed.

VS 367 SMALL FACES: Tin Soldier/Tin Soldier (Live)/Rene

Rel: 18 Jul 1980[1] **Del:** 1981[6] **RRP:** £1.15[8]

Two tracks on b–side. Only solid–centred copies confirmed. Not issued in picture sleeve. This is the only place, apart from the pointlessly–rare *In Memorium* LP, that the live version of *Tin Soldier* exists on UK vinyl.

CAMBRA

Both releases were licensed from Zeema Records and were issued in single sleeves despite being double albums. Cassette issues comprised two separate cassettes. The documented 1985 release dates are most likely redistribution dates following a move to K-Tel/Conifer after IDM, the original distributor, ceased trading.

CR 000 sequence double LP

CR 086 ***VARIOUS ARTISTS: Psychadelic Smashes***

Record 1: side 1
1. Itchycoo Park (Small Faces)
2. (If Paradise Is) Half As Nice (Amen Corner)
3. Paint It Black (Chris Farlowe)
4. Thoughts Of Emerlist Davjack (The Nice)
5. First Cut Is The Deepest (P.P. Arnold)
6. Hang On Sloopy (The McCoys)
7. Tin Soldier (Small Faces)

Record 1: side 2
1. The Universal (Small Faces)
2. The Time Has Come (P.P. Arnold)
3. Hello Suzie (Amen Corner)
4. All Or Nothing (Small Faces)
5. Fever (The McCoys)
6. America (The Nice)

Rel: May 1985[9]
RRP: £2.99

Record 2: side 1
1. Out Of Time (Chris Farlowe)
2. Sitting On A Fence (Twice As Much)
3. Get Back (Amen Corner)
4. Here Comes The Nice (Small Faces)
5. Natural Born Bugie (Humble Pie)
6. (If You Think You're) Groovy (P.P. Arnold)
7. Think (Chris Farlowe)

Record 2: side 2
1. Man Of The World (Fleetwood Mac)
2. Angel Of The Morning (P.P. Arnold)
3. Bend Me, Shape Me (Amen Corner)
4. Lazy Sunday (Small Faces)
5. Handbags And Gladrags (Chris Farlowe)
6. Farewell To The Real Magnificent Seven (Amen Corner)

Cassette: CRT 086 **Rel:** May 1985[9]
Title spelling as above. Labels have 1983 issue date, which most likely represents the original release.

CR 5100 sequence double LP

CR 5162 ***VARIOUS ARTISTS: Legends***

Rel: Mar 1985[9]
RRP: £2.99

Record 1: side 1

1. Telephone Blues (John Mayall And The Bluesbreakers)
2. You Don't Love Me (T.S. McPhee)
3. West Coast Idea (Eric Clapton)
4. Ain't Seen No Whiskey (Jo–Ann Kelly)
5. Flapjacks (Stone's Masonry)
6. Cold Blooded Woman (Savoy Brown Blues Band)

Record 1: side 2

1. On Top Of The World (John Mayall And The Bluesbreakers)
2. Someone To Love Me (T.S. McPhee)
3. Can't Quit You Baby (Savoy Brown Blues Band)
4. Draggin' My Tail (Eric Clapton With Jimmy Page)
5. Dealing With The Devil (Dharma Blues Band)
6. Who's Knocking (Jeremy Spencer)

Record 2: side 1

1. Freight Loader (Eric Clapton And Jimmy Page)
2. Look Down Down At My Woman (Jeremy Spencer)
3. Roll 'Em Pete (Dharma Blues Band)
4. Choker (Eric Clapton And Jimmy Page)
5. True Blue (Savoy Brown Brown Blues Band)
6. When You Got A Good Friend (T.S. McPhee)

Record 2: side 2

1. I'm Your Witchdoctor (John Mayall And The Bluesbreakers)
2. Snake Drive (Eric Clapton)
3. Ain't Gonna Cry No More (T.S. McPhee)
4. I Tried (Savoy Brown Blues Band)
5. Tribute To Elmore (Eric Clapton)
6. I Feel So Good (Jo–Ann Kelly)

Cassette: CRT 5162 **Rel:** Mar 1985[9]

Some sleeves mis–cut with spine credits showing sideways on the front, part of the Cambra logo truncated and off–bleed area showing on the back of the sleeve. Labels have 1984 issue date, which most likely represents the original release, 1985 being the redistribution date. Side 1 is a straight reissue of side 2 of IMLP 014 and side 1 of IMAL 05/06; side 2 is a straight reissue of side 1 of IMCP 015 and side 3 of IMAL 05/06; side 3 is a straight reissue of side 2 of IMCP 015 and side 4 of IMAL 03/04; side 4 is a straight reissue of side 1 of IMLP 014 and side 1 of IMAL 03/04.

OLD GOLD

Perhaps it's not surprising that these Immediate gems took so long to find themselves licensed to this specialist golden oldies reissue label. After all, NEMS had spent the last ten years trying to get full mileage out of the Immediate catalogue with their own multiple reissues. The assumption is that the belated licensing of these tracks was down to the new owners – all labels include the text, "Issued under licence from Interworld Communications (Records) Ltd." which sounds suspiciously like a Castle Communications spin–off. No doubt this was a good way to quickly recoup some of its recent investment in NEMS (note that OG 9467 was a Black Sabbath pairing).

The pairing of the Fleetwood Mac and Humble Pie hits on one single and the pairing of The McCoys' *Hang On Sloopy* with *Fever* are not included because both were released in September 1985[9] whilst this discography stops dead at midnight, 19 August 1985.

OG 9000 sequence 7" singles

OG 9464 ***P. P. ARNOLD: The First Cut Is The Deepest/Angel Of The Morning***

Rel: Jan 1985[9]

Exists on two label designs, the second from (probably) September 1985, so just outside the period covered in this discography. The original label design has a curved scroll logo.

OG 9465 ***SMALL FACES: Lazy Sunday/Tin Soldier***

Rel: Jan 1985[9]

Exists on two label designs, details as per OG 9464.

OG 9466 ***SMALL FACES: Itchycoo Park/Here Comes The Nice***

Rel: Jan 1985[9]

The company sleeve accompanying this release (and probably the other three releases as well) advertised *Itchycoo Park* as being available on the label. Thanks to an interesting placement of the Old Gold logo, it also advertises "radise Is) Half As Nice".

OG 9468 ***CHRIS FARLOWE: Out Of Time/Think***

Rel: Jan 1985[9]

Exists on two label designs, details as per OG 9464.

OG 9469 ***AMEN CORNER: (If Paradise Is) Half As Nice/Hello Suzie***

Rel: Jan 1985[9]

RECORDS THAT NEVER WERE

Note that the Mike D'Abo single, *Gulliver's Travels (See The Little People)*, is not included here because copies were pressed and issued, even if the single was subsequently withdrawn. The same goes for the *Gulliver's Travels* LP on Instant.

Singles that never were

IM ??? ***JULIAN PROTEST QUINTET: Satisfaction/Like A Bob Dylan***

Simon Spence's *Immediate* book states that Immediate pressed up copies of this instrumental version of the Stones' hit, backed with a response to Dylan's *Like A Rolling Stone*. Spence's book, however, seems to be the only place to document this.

IM ??? ***THE ARANBEE POP SYMPHONY ORCHESTRA: Unknown Track/ Unknown Track***

Planned release: 11 Feb 1966

News of the impending release of this single was documented in the 5, February 1966 edition of the *Billboard* trade magazine. No such single was subsequently issued.

IM ??? ***SAM COOKE: That's Heaven To Me/Unknown Track***

Planned release: 11 Feb 1966

News of the impending release of this single was documented in the 5, February 1966 edition of the *Billboard* trade magazine. No such single was subsequently issued.

IM ??? ***SMALL FACES: Mystery/Unknown Track***

Planned release: 1967

Intended as a single but only made it as far as an acetate for Andrew Oldham to check the mix. It was later issued on the first album under the title of *Somerthing I Want To Tell You* with a re–recorded vocal track. A replica copy of the acetate was issued as part of the lavish, multi–media box set *Here Come The Nice* (Immediate/Sanctuary), which was not for sale in UK (unless you had £212 spare and an overseas accomodation address, that is).

IM ??? ***BILLY NICHOLLS: It Brings Me Down/Unknown Track***

This is documented in Simon Spence's *Immediate* book as being the planned follow up to *Would You Believe*. The book states that Immediate had even put together a film to promote it but lack of sales of the LP led to the single's cancellation.

IM 067 ***OUTER LIMITS: Great Train Robbery/Sweet Freedom***

Planned release: 10 May 1968

Strictly speaking, this is not a record that never was because demos exist, though no stock copies were pressed. A different version was issued on Instant, as IN 001, in September 1968. This catalogue number was reassigned to P.P. Arnold's *Angel Of The Morning*.

IM ??? ***P.P. ARNOLD: Would You Believe/Am I Still Dreaming***
German copies in picture sleeve exist and the unused IM 083 catalogue number has been mooted as having been intended for this coupling. However, it looks more as though this was chosen for release in Germany instead of a second issue of *The First Cut Is The Deepest* in March 1969.

IM ??? ***HUMBLE PIE: The Sad Bag Of Shaky Jake/Cold Lady***
According to Simon Spence's *Immediate* book, promotional copies of this were pressed and sent out in the UK, which is perfectly possible, but has anyone ever seen one? The b–side is a best guess based on the fact that this coupling was issued in several other countries, including France, Germany, Holland and New Zealand.

IM ??? ***THE NICE: Hang On To A Dream/Diary Of An Empty Day***
Issued in Holland and Germany in December 1969 (45cat.com). Perhaps also planned for UK issue but swallowed up in Immediate's collapse. Who knows? Included for neatness only!

IMS 100 ***SMALL FACES: Tin Soldier/I Feel Much Better***
Rel: supposedly 1976
My best guess is this supposed NEMS/Immediate single started life as a typo in the *Record Collector Rare Record Price Guide 2000*. Confirmed issue is IMS 110.

Albums that never were

Liberty: ***DEL SHANNON: Home And Away***

1. It's My Feeling
2. Mind Over Matter
3. Silently
4. Cut And Come Again
5. My Love Has Gone

1. Led Along
2. Life Is But Nothing
3. Easy To Say Easy To Do
4. Friendly With You
5. He Cheated
6. Runaway (aka Runaway '67)

Recorded at Olympic Studios in February 1967, produced by Andrew Oldham. Tracks include three compositions each by Immediate songwriters, Billy Nicholls, Andrew Rose and David Skinner. Five tracks were issued on single in various territories, but the rest remained unissued until 1978, when fourteen tracks from the sessions were issued on Sunset as *And The Music Plays On* (SRS 50412).

Del Shannon was under contract to Liberty and various singles from the sessions were issued on that label; Oldham was contracted in his guise of independent record producer and the LP is included here purely because it was an Immediate Production, though not for release on Immediate.

The Billy Nicholls–written *Led Along* was issued as the a–side of a single in the US (Liberty, 55961) with the b–side taken from different sessions. The new version of *Runaway* was issued with *He Cheated*, both from the Oldham sessions, in the US (Liberty, 55993). The UK version of *Runaway* (Liberty, LBF 15020) included a different, non–Oldham produced, b–side. *Led Along* was relegated to a b–side in the UK, with *Mind Over Matter*, another track from the Oldham sessions, on the a–side (Liberty, LIB 10277). Possibly the real oddity is that one track from the sessions, *Silently*, found itself issued as a b–side to a non–Oldham produced track in the Phillipines (Liberty, LB–20376). All single releases were mono versions, whilst the album was recorded in stereo. All bar the Phillipines single credit either "An Immediate Production" or "An Immediate (Ldn.) Prod." Well, apart from the US release of *Led Along*, which has the exteremely ungrammatical "A Immediate Productions".

Immediate: ***THE SMALL FACES: 1862***

1. The Autumn Stone
2. Red Balloon
3. Collibosher
4. Buttermilk Boy

1. Pig Trotters
2. Picaninny
3. Wide Eyed Girl On The Wall
4. Donkey Rides, A Penny A Glass
5. War Of The Worlds

The above assumes the order as documented by Toby Marriott (see below) to be 'correct' (even though conjectural) and is further based on timings of tracks so as to come up with around the same overall timing per side. *Pig Trotters* (aka *The Pig Trotters*) resurfaced as *Wrist Job*, recorded by Humble Pie, who also recorded *Buttermilk Boy*.

Some tracks already recorded for the album appeared instead on both *The Autumn Stone* and *In Memorium*. Presumably, some of those issued as instrumentals would have had vocals added prior to release had the group not split up. As to the intended track listing, Steve Marriott's son, Toby, has the following to say (sourced, with minor corrections, from http://musiccornershop.blogspot.co.uk/2008/02/complete–red–balloon–story–by–mick.html; accessed 11, May 2014):

> My curiosity started after I was given a songbook dad owned circa 1968 that had possible idea's for the Ogden's follow up...
>
> 1. The Autumn Stone; 2.Red Balloon; 3.Colibosher; 4.Buttermilk Boy; 5.Pig Trotters/Wrist Job; 6. Picaninny; 7. Wide Eyed Girl On The Wall; 8. Donkey Rides, A Penny, A Glass; 9. There was a reference to a song simply noted as "blues jam" I think this later turned out as War Of The Worlds.
>
> Unfortunately the songbook got stolen some years ago so I'm trying to remember offhand. If you put in consideration the songs Plonk wrote for 'First Step' then to me you've got a blinder of a follow up! Shame it never happened...

There are some interesting versions of some of the above tracks available on both CD and on various vinyl issues from down the years. For those that want to get as 'close to the source' as possible, then, apart from *The Autumn Stone* double album or *In Memorium* single album (and the b–side to *The Universal*, of course), there are four LPs to hunt out, two US releases, one Italian release and one German release. Three of these albums fail to mention the Small Faces and present the records as Rod Stewart albums.

The US 1977 LP, *Rod Stewart And The Faces* (Springboard, SPB–4030), includes the following tracks (titles as included on the LP): *A Collibosher*; *The Fly*; *Anything*; *Sparkey Rides*; *Wide Eyed Girl*; *Red Balloon*; *Autumn Stone*. The other two tracks are *Just A Little Misunderstood* and *Baby Come Home*, so you only got two tracks with Rod Stewart if you bought this. True, you did get three of The Faces on the rest of the tracks.

As regards the actual tracks: *Collibosher* has no evidence of flute; *The Fly* is an instrumental version of *The Hungry Intruder*; *Anyway* is an instrumental run through of *Tin Soldier* with no guitar; *Sparkey Rides* is an awful cacophony of *Donkey Rides, A Penny A Glass*, which appears to be close to the version as released but with two competing bass lines, as though someone failed to keep the faders down on a discarded (and very out of time) rehearsal bass track; *Wide Eyed Girl* isn't *Wide–Eyed Girl On The Wall*, but is a version of *Wham Bam, Thank You Man*; *Red Balloon* is near complete, with vocals, but obviously isn't the version as released; *Autumn Stone* has flute from the very start and sounds like a rough mix of the version as released.

The US 1977 LP, *Rod Stewart And Steampacket* (Springboard, SPB–4063), includes just *Wide–Eyed Girl* (which gets a dash added for this release and is also credited as being 8 seconds shorter than on the previous album) and *Red Balloon*. As above, *Wide–Eyed Girl* is, again, really *Wham Bam, Thank You Man* and sounds to be exactly the same as the 'longer' version on the previous Springboard album.

The Italian 1982 LP, *Ridin' High Vol 1* (Joker, SM 3985) includes *Sparky Rides* (without "e" this time and with an incorrect track timing of 2.09 instead of 3.09), *Wild Eyed Girl* (yes, "Wild") and *Red Balloon*. It looks, though, that *Wild Eyed Girl* really is *Wide–Eyed Girl On The Wall* this time. I've not managed to find a copy of this album to listen to yet, but the supposition that *Wide–Eyed Girl On The Wall* is included is down to the fact that the next album to be considered says so.

The German 1984 LP, *Rarities* (Line/Outline, OLLP 5283), pulls together all of the above tracks and gives them their correct names. It also manages to get all of the Immediate era tracks onto one side of an LP (all of the other LPs mentioned come in at 15 minutes a side or less). The other side is made up of tracks from the, at that point unavailable, *In The Begining* Decca/Teldec LP.

Other titles from BFP that you are bound to like!

Find out more about these and other books from:
www.bristol–folk.co.uk **and/or** ***www.lulu.com/spotlight/vinylattic***

Transacord: Sounds of Steam – with free CD

The Famous Charisma Discography

The Saydisc & Village Thing Discography

Bristol Folk: a discographical history

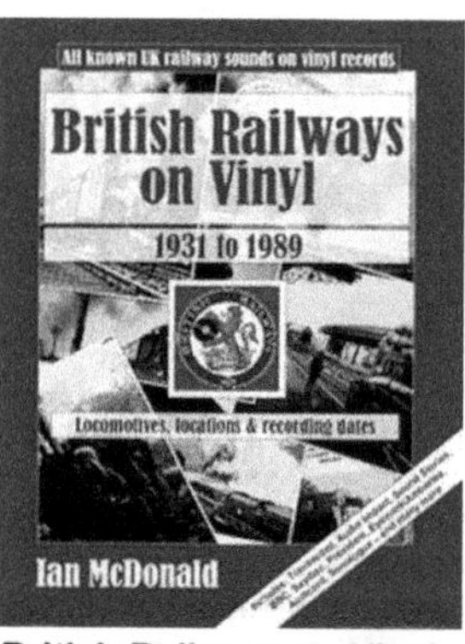

British Railways on Vinyl: Ian McDonald's magnum opus

The B&C Discography (Award-Nominated)

The Virgin Discography The 1970s

...and for those that want to document their entire record collection, what you need is a database...

www.ingramcontent.com/pod-product-compliance
Ingram Content Group UK Ltd.
Pitfield, Milton Keynes, MK11 3LW, UK
UKHW020344250726
13967UKWH00005B/2101